Science Concepts SECOND SERIES

Matter

Alvin Silverstein, Virginia Silverstein,
and Laura Silverstein Nunn

 Twenty-First Century Books
Minneapolis

Twenty-First Century Books
A division of Lerner Publishing Group, Inc.
241 First Avenue North
Minneapolis, MN 55401 U.S.A.

Website address: www.lernerbooks.com

Library of Congress Cataloging-in-Publication Data

Silverstein, Alvin.
    Matter / by Alvin Silverstein, Virginia Silverstein, Laura Silverstein Nunn.
       p. cm. — (Science concepts : second series)
    Includes bibliographical references and index.
    ISBN 978-0-8225-7515-3 (lib. bdg. : alk. paper)
    1. Matter—Properties—Juvenile literature. I. Silverstein, Virginia B.
 II. Nunn, Laura Silverstein. III. Title.
 QC173.36.S555 2009
 530—dc22   2007049493

Manufactured in the United States of America
1 2 3 4 5 6 – DP – 14 13 12 11 10 09

Contents

What's the Matter?

What do you have in your bedroom? If you're like most kids, your parents are constantly telling you to clean up all your stuff. Maybe you left video games lying on the floor. The dust on your bookshelf is starting to make you sneeze. And when you tossed your dirty clothes in the direction of the hamper, you missed it entirely.

You probably don't think twice about all the stuff you have in your room or about the things in your family's house. All these things and, in fact, everything in the universe—from a tiny speck of dust on your bedroom floor to the stars far, far away in our galaxy—is made of matter. Everything you can see, touch, or smell—and even things you can't—is made of matter. You and your family and friends are also made of matter. But what is matter?

People use the word *matter* in many different ways. For example, if something's wrong, we might ask, "What's the matter?" Or we might tell a friend, "We have some important matters to talk about." In science the word *matter* has a very specific meaning. It is something that takes up space and has mass. In other words, it has resistance to being moved.

Everything that exists in the universe, from the socks on your bedroom floor to the air you breathe, is made of matter.

Mass is a measure of the amount of matter in an object. In everyday speech, people often refer to mass as weight. For example, it takes a lot more effort to pick up a heavy rock than to pick up a piece of paper.

It is easy to picture a baseball bat, the sand in a sandbox, or a bucketful of water as being made of matter. But what about air? You can't see it or smell it (unless, for example, there is somebody wearing perfume or an open garbage can nearby), and you can't feel it unless the wind is blowing. Air *is* made of matter, though. The individual bits of matter in air are too tiny to see. There are so few of them in the volume of air around you that they weigh hardly anything at all.

"Which is heavier, a pound of feathers or a pound of lead?" That old joke is a trick question, of course. A pound (0.5 kilogram) of anything weighs exactly as much as a pound of anything else. But the feathers would make a huge pile, while a lead bar with the same weight is small enough to hold in your hand.

Actually, there are several ways of measuring how much of something there is. In addition to weight (or mass), there is also volume—the amount of space something takes up. In the United States, people use the English system of measurement. Weights are given in pounds or ounces. Volumes may be measured in gallons, quarts, pints, cups, fluid ounces, tablespoons, and teaspoons.

The amount of matter (mass) in a unit of volume is called its density. Different kinds of matter have different densities, depending on what they are made of. The higher the density, the more matter is packed into the same volume and the heavier the object will be. For this reason, a wooden baseball bat that a major leaguer uses is much

However, most of the world—and all the world's scientists— use the metric system of measurement. Weight is measured in kilograms, grams, and smaller fractions of grams. The metric units for volume are liters, milliliters, and so on.

Here are some common conversions of English to metric measurements:

Mass (Weight)
1 ounce (oz.) = 28 grams
8 ounces = 227 g
1 pound (lb.) = 0.45 kg
2.2 pounds = 1 kg

Liquid Volume
1 teaspoon = 5 milliliters
1 tablespoon = 15 ml
1 fluid ounce = 30 ml
1 cup = 240 ml
1 pint = 480 ml
1 quart = 0.95 liters
1 gallon = 3.8 liters

heavier than an aluminum bat and a baseball is much heavier than a foam ball.

What Makes Up Matter?

If a baseball bat, a bucket of water, and a roomful of air are all made of matter, then why are they so different? They are

Scientist Melvin Calvin holds a model of the sucrose molecule that he used in his study of sugar structure. The balls represent the atoms, and the sticks represent the bonds joining the atoms together.

different because they are made of different kinds of particles.

Everything that exists is made up of many tiny particles, each one too small to see—even with an ordinary microscope. The particles in matter are called atoms, and about one hundred different kinds of atoms exist. Some substances, such as pure gold, are made of just one kind of atom—gold atoms. But in most things, different kinds of atoms are joined together like the parts of a Tinkertoy. These joined atoms form larger particles called molecules. (Molecules may be larger than atoms, but they are still too small to see without a very good microscope.)

Each kind of atom has its own set of rules determining what other atoms it can join with and how they connect to become a molecule. Pure water is made of just one kind of molecule (water molecules). But most substances—such as the wood in a baseball bat—are mixtures of a number of different kinds of molecules. The wood in a baseball bat is made up mainly of large and complicated molecules called cellulose and lignins. The wood in a living tree also contains quite a bit of water, along with sugars, salts, and other molecules. The following chapters will take a closer look into the matter that makes up our universe.

States of Matter

Did you have your matter for breakfast? Did you drink a glass of matter today? Do you carry your matter to school with you? What kind of matter do you like on your pizza?

The cereal you ate for breakfast and the milk you drank were all made of matter. Your backpack and the books inside it are matter too. So is the cheese on your pizza and even the air you breathe. As you can see, matter can take on different forms, or states. Three main states of matter exist. Matter can be a solid, such as a book or a bowl of cereal. It can be a liquid, such as water or milk. Or it can be a gas, such as air or steam.

The different states of matter depend on how closely atoms and molecules are packed together. In a solid, the particles are packed together tightly. In a liquid, the particles are more loosely packed, and in a gas, the particles are quite far apart with a lot of empty space between them.

Atoms and molecules are in constant motion. The more space between them, the more they can move around. The temperature of matter is linked to the motion of its atoms and molecules: the faster they move, the higher the temperature of the matter.

The Extreme States

Many people are familiar with the matter that comes in solid, liquid, and gas forms. But there are actually *five* states of matter altogether. The other two states are known as plasma and Bose-Einstein condensates (BEC). Scientists consider these extreme states of matter. They do not usually exist in our everyday lives.

Plasma is a gas that forms at extremely hot temperatures. It is commonly found in outer space in the stars and in the center of the Sun. (The Sun's center heats up to millions of degrees.) On Earth, plasma is formed in the air by lightning during an electrical storm. It's also found in man-made objects, such as fluorescent lightbulbs and neon signs. These lights are made of long tubes filled with a gas such as neon or argon. Plasma forms when electricity hits the gas inside the tube. The plasma in a plasma TV set is formed in a similar way. It is used to produce a bright, clear picture on a large flat screen.

On the other hand, BECs form at extremely cold temperatures. The coldest temperature possible—with no heat at all—is known as absolute zero. BECs form when the temperature is a few billionths of a degree above absolute zero. (Scientists do not believe it is possible to cool a substance to absolute zero.)

States of Matter

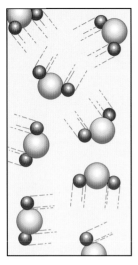 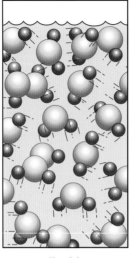 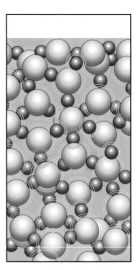

gas   liquid   solid

In a gas state, particles have a lot of room to move about. In a liquid state, molecules are closer together but still move freely. In a solid state, molecules are tightly packed and hardly move at all.

In general, a substance is in the solid state at low temperatures, in the liquid state at higher temperatures, and in a gas state at even higher temperatures. The particular temperatures at which matter passes from one state into another depend on the substance.

What Is a Solid?

A solid has a definite shape and volume. Volume is the amount of space a substance or object takes up. It takes

In order for a solid to change shape, it must be acted upon by an outside force, such as an ax splitting a block of wood.

effort to change the shape of a solid—such as sawing a block of wood in half or heating it until it catches fire.

Solids can have many different properties. A solid can be hard like a block of wood or soft like a pillow. Its surface may be rough like sandpaper or smooth like silk. It can be strong like steel, brittle (easily broken) like an eggshell, or crumbly like sand. It can be heavy like a rock or very light like a feather. It can be stiff like a tabletop or stretchy like a rubber band. Some solids are transparent (see-through), while others are not. For example, you can see what's inside a plastic food storage bag, but not what's inside a paper bag.

Did You Know?
Movement creates heat. The more movement there is in a substance, the warmer it is. And without any movement, heat doesn't exist at all. For example, at absolute zero (-459.67°F, or -273.15°C), atoms and molecules would not move at all.

How can solids be so different from each other? Their characteristics depend on the atoms and molecules that form them and how these atoms and molecules are put together. In a solid, the particles are held together tightly, usually in a regular pattern that repeats itself again and again. The particles can jiggle a little bit, but they do not move very much. Because they are so tightly packed, each one is kept in place by the atoms or molecules around it. That is why a solid will keep its shape—unless a physical force changes it. For

What Are Crystals?

The atoms or molecules that form many solids are joined together in a regular pattern, forming flat sheets, cubes, or more complex 3-D structures. These solids are in a crystal form. Diamonds are crystals, and if you look at salt or sugar under a magnifying glass, you can see that they are crystalline too.

Not all solids are crystalline, though. Some are what scientists call amorphous solids. (*Amorphous* comes from Greek words meaning "without shape.") Their atoms or molecules are jumbled together randomly, without forming any regular pattern. Glass is an amorphous solid. Many plastics are amorphous too.

example, if you take a bite out of an apple, you are using the force of your teeth to change its shape.

Because the particles are packed together so tightly, solids cannot be compressed (squeezed) to a smaller volume. A collection of bicycle parts will not change its volume, even after the parts are put together to form a new shape. The bike will keep the same volume, whether it is put together or in parts. The mass of the bike parts stays the same, as well. So does the density. (Remember that the density is the amount of mass in a unit of volume. Since both the mass and the volume have not changed, the density stays the same.)

What Is a Liquid?

Unlike solids, liquids do not have a definite shape. If you pour milk into a glass, it will take the shape of the glass. But if you knock the glass over, the milk will spill onto the tabletop and spread out over the surface. Now the milk looks

A liquid takes the shape of the container it's in. When spilled, it spreads out over the surface.

like a liquid blob—the glass is no longer giving it shape.

Even though water, ketchup, and maple syrup are all liquids, they are different from one another in the ways they look, feel, and behave.

All liquids flow, and they can take the shape of the container they are in. Liquids do have their differences, though—in the way they look and in the way they feel. A liquid can be thin, like water or gasoline, or it can be thick, like ketchup, shampoo, or a milk shake. A liquid can feel slippery, like cooking or motor oil, or it can feel sticky, like honey or maple syrup.

Liquids also differ in how fast they can flow. For example, water flows very quickly, as you can easily see by turning on a water faucet. But try pouring maple syrup on your pancakes or ketchup on your french fries. You can see that these liquids take a bit more time flowing out of their containers.

Experiment: How Fast Is the Flow?

Different kinds of liquids flow at different speeds. You can see this for yourself by doing a little experiment. You will need a pencil, two Styrofoam cups, a watch or clock that shows seconds, a large bowl, vegetable oil, and maple syrup.

Using a pencil, punch a small hole in the bottom of each cup. Then fill one cup with water, while covering the hole with your finger. Hold the cup over the sink and take your finger off the hole. Use a watch or clock to time how long it takes for all the water to flow out of the cup. Write down the number. Then fill the same cup with vegetable oil. (Remember to put your finger over the hole first.) Place a bowl underneath the cup of oil. Remove your finger and record the amount of time it takes for the oil to flow into the bowl.

Next, fill the second cup with maple syrup (while plugging the hole with your finger). Place a bowl underneath the cup of maple syrup and remove your finger. Record how long it takes for the maple syrup to flow out of the cup. Which liquid—water, vegetable oil, or maple syrup—flowed the fastest? Which was the slowest?

In a liquid, the particles are fairly close together, but they have more room to move about than in solids. In fact, they are moving around all the time. Their movements are random, without any kind of pattern. The particles are constantly changing positions, as each one slides around another. This action allows the liquid to flow, as it takes the shape of its container.

Like solids, liquids cannot be compressed (pressed into a smaller space) because the particles are close together. So their volume remains the same. If you pour a cupful of water into a glass and then pour the glass of water into a larger container, the amounts may look different, but that's because of the size of the containers. The water can spread out more in a large jug, and it does not rise as high as in the glass. But you still have only a single cupful of water—there is no change in volume.

The density of liquids varies. The most common liquids in our world are water and mixtures of water with small amounts of other things, such as orange juice, milk, and shampoo. Blood is mostly water too. We tend to expect liquids to have a density similar to that of water. But some liquids, such as cooking oil and cleaning fluid, are less dense than water (weigh less than the same amount of water). And mercury, the only metal that is liquid at room temperature (around 68°F, or 20°C), is *much* denser than water. You will get a big surprise if you try to lift a beaker full of mercury.

What Is a Gas?

The air you breathe is a mixture of gases. It is invisible. It has no shape or size. (But it can take the shape of a balloon if you blow air into it.) Most of the time, you don't even notice the air around you unless the wind blows.

In a gas, the particles are very spread out. They move around really fast, bouncing around like Ping-Pong balls. They are not arranged in any

Filling a balloon with air helps us see how gas expands to fill the shape of the container it is in.

kind of pattern. They are constantly changing positions, shooting around in all different directions and knocking against one another.

Gases can do something that solids and liquids cannot do. They can change their volume. If you remove a gas from a small container and release it into a larger container, the gas will expand to fill in the extra space. How does that happen? Do new molecules suddenly appear? Do the molecules get bigger? No. The number of molecules does not change, nor does their size. The molecules simply spread out. So the only thing that increases is the amount of space between the molecules.

Since gas particles are so far apart, they are easy to compress—unlike solids and liquids. For example, the air inside a scuba tank is compressed, so the tank can actually hold more air than a rubber balloon of the same volume.

Changing States of Matter

What happens if you take an ice cube out of the freezer and place it on a plate at room temperature? After an hour, the solid ice cube has become nothing more than a puddle of water. The ice melted. The three states of matter we encounter every day—solids, liquids, and gases—can change from one state to another when they are exposed to either very low or very high temperatures.

An ice cube is simply frozen water. Liquids such as water become frozen when their temperature reaches a certain point, called the freezing point. The freezing point of water is 32°F (0°C). As the temperature drops, the molecules lose energy. Energy is the ability to do work. Molecules have less energy and move more slowly in colder temperatures. Eventually they slow down so much that

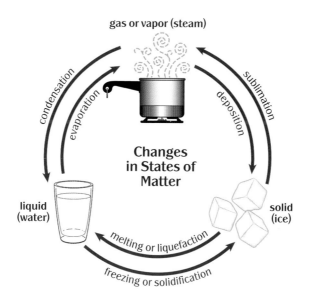

Changes in the state of matter are reversible. Solids can melt to form liquids, which may evaporate into the gas state or freeze into the solid state. Gases can be condensed to form liquids. Matter can also move directly from the solid to the gas state (sublimation) and back again (deposition).

the water becomes a solid. Other liquids with a different chemical composition (that is, made of different atoms or molecules) each have their own freezing points, at which their state changes to a solid. Whole milk, for example, freezes at about 31°F (−0.54°C). Honey freezes at about 29°F (−1.5°C). And rubbing alcohol freezes at a much lower temperature: −117°F (−83°C).

When an ice cube is left out at room temperature, the molecules gain energy as the ice gets warmer. The warmer the ice cube gets, the more energy the molecules have to move around. Eventually, the solid ice cube will melt into liquid water. The point at which a solid turns into a liquid is called its melting point. The melting point may be different for different types of matter. Some substances need higher temperatures than others to turn into a liquid.

Antifreeze

People add antifreeze to a car's radiator to keep the water in the radiator from freezing in the winter. Antifreeze is a mixture of water and chemicals that have a lower freezing point than water. The mixture stays liquid far below water's freezing point of 32°F (0°C). For example, the antifreeze commonly sold in the United States protects the engine down to −40°F (−40°C). In most places, that temperature is low enough to keep the car running all through the winter.

When water is heated to 212°F (100°C), it will start to boil. The molecules inside the boiling water are moving really fast. They are moving so fast that many of them break away from the others. As they rise into the air, they take the form of a gas (steam). Scientists call this the boiling point—the point at which a liquid becomes a gas. If you look at a pot of water boiling on the stove, you can see wisps of steam rising from the pot.

Actually, water can turn into a gas, or evaporate, long before

When water is heated to 212°F (100°C), the molecules break away from the liquid state, forming steam.

it reaches the boiling point. That happens at the surface of the water, which is in contact with the air. Since the molecules in liquid water are constantly moving, some of them escape from the liquid surface and enter the air as a gas, called water vapor. This happens even at room temperature, but more water evaporates as the temperature rises. For example, does your bathroom get all steamed up when you take a shower? When you are done, the temperature in the room starts to cool down. Then water droplets form on the walls. The water vapor condensed when it hit the cool wall, turning back into liquid water. (People

Dry Ice

What makes those spooky vapors that add "atmosphere" at a rock concert? It's a change in state of a rather common kind of matter existing in a very *uncommon* form: solid carbon dioxide, or dry ice.

Normally carbon dioxide is a colorless gas, which makes up a small part of the air in Earth's atmosphere. Our bodies produce carbon dioxide when we burn food for energy. It is in the air we breathe out. It also makes the bubbles in carbonated soft drinks. Carbon dioxide gas turns

often call a mist of water vapor "steam," but scientists and engineers use the word *steam* only for the very hot gas form of water, above its boiling point.)

Molecules in water can even evaporate from the surface of solid ice, below the freezing point of water! That is how a sheet of ice on a winter sidewalk gradually disappears. (The evaporation of a solid directly into a gas is called sublimation.)

Changes in state all involve an increase or decrease in energy. To melt a solid or evaporate a liquid, you need to add energy. The heat of the stove, for example, provides the energy to boil water. The energy from sunlight heats up an icy sidewalk and causes some of the ice to melt into liquid water

into a solid at –109°F (–78.5°C). If you expose this dry ice to room temperature, it does not melt. It gradually sublimes, that is, goes directly from the solid into the gas state. This gas state is visible and looks like fog. The spooky vapors you see at a rock concert are really subliming dry ice.

Dry ice stays cold at room temperature longer than ice made from water, which melts. Because it stays cold longer, dry ice is sometimes used in coolers to keep food from spoiling. It is also used in movies to make artificial snow. It is called "dry" ice because no water or liquid is involved.

and some to evaporate into the air. When matter changes its state in the opposite direction—a gas condensing into a liquid or a liquid into a solid—it releases some energy.

When water freezes into ice or boils into steam, is it still water? Actually, yes. Changes in the state of matter do not change its chemical nature. The changes are reversible—they can also go in the opposite direction if the conditions are right. You can get liquid water back by cooling steam and by heating ice. Scientists call this kind of change a physical change.

Chemical changes are quite different. They actually change the nature of a substance. Some chemical changes are reversible too, but many are not. For example, when wood is burned, its complicated carbon compounds are chemically changed into simpler products such as carbon dioxide and water vapor (gases), and some solid ashes. You can't put those gases and ashes back together to make a log of wood again.

Burning wood changes its chemical nature by reacting with oxygen to give two new products—carbon dioxide and water.

Hot and Sweaty

Your body has its own built-in cooling systems, which can keep you from heating up when it is hot outside. Your blood (which is mostly water) carries heat out to your skin, where the heat can pass out into the air.

How does this work? Some of the water from your blood passes into sweat glands in the skin, which open to the skin's surface through tiny holes called pores. The water evaporates as it passes out of the sweat pores, cooling you. (Evaporating water gets rid of a lot of heat.) Moisture also evaporates from the inner lining of your lungs each time you exhale.

So why do you feel so hot and sweaty when the humidity is high? Humidity is the amount of water vapor already in the air, due to evaporation from oceans, ponds, and streams, as well as from people and animals exhaling. When the humidity is high, the air cannot hold much more water vapor. So instead of evaporating, your sweat stays in the liquid form and spreads over your body surface. Instead of feeling cool, you feel wet and sticky.

Water, the Strange Matter

What happens when you drop an ice cube into a glass of water? It rises to the top and floats. So what's so strange about that? Well, only things that are lighter (less dense) than water can float in it. That means that ice must be lighter than water. But most liquids get heavier (denser) when they turn into solids. This unusual characteristic of water has some interesting and important effects in the real world. The water at the top of a pond, for example, always freezes first as the weather gets cold in the winter. The colder it gets, the thicker the layer of ice gets as more water freezes. Because ice is lighter than water, it always stays at the top. Usually some of the water, in the deeper parts of the pond, stays liquid. That's because the layer of ice acts as insulation, holding in some warmth. Fish can swim in the water under the ice, and animals such as frogs can snuggle down in the mud at the bottom of the pond and survive all winter long.

Fish in this pond are swimming under a layer of ice. When liquid water freezes, its molecules form a solid that is less dense than its liquid state.

Water not only gets lighter when it freezes, it also expands (its volume increases). If you put a full bottle of juice in the freezer, the water in the juice may freeze, expand, and crack the bottle. Cracks in sidewalks and potholes in roads form in a similar way. Water that is trapped inside thin cracks freezes in the winter. As it expands, it forces the sides of the crack apart and makes bigger holes.

Cracks in a sidewalk can form when water in a small crack freezes. As the freezing water expands, it forces the crack to get bigger.

Another unique property of water is that under certain conditions it can become superheated (staying liquid above its boiling point) or supercooled (staying liquid below its freezing point). These "super" states are unstable—they can break down suddenly. When you heat a cup of water in a microwave oven, for example, it may become superheated. If you take the cup out and pour in some instant tea or coffee—boom! The water starts to boil furiously and may explode out of the cup. You can avoid a burn by tapping the side of the cup with a spoon before taking it out of the microwave. That helps to shake up the boiling liquid and keeps it from superheating. (To avoid superheating in the first place, be sure not to heat the water too long.)

"What is the world made of?" is an age-old question.

About twenty-five hundred years ago, a Greek scientist

named Democritus was among the first to provide

an explanation. All the things on Earth, he explained,

are made of extremely tiny, simple particles. He called

them atoms. These atoms can combine and rearrange

themselves to form trees, stones, ships, sails, frogs,

and even human beings. These things may die or wear

away, but atoms go on forever.

It was an interesting theory, but very few people believed him at the time. Democritus could not prove his theory. Nor could any other scientists prove their ideas about what the world was made of. It took more than two thousand years before anyone could show the existence of atoms and molecules.

What Are Atoms Made Of?

As small as atoms are, these tiny particles contain particles that are even tinier. Atoms are made up of three main kinds of particles: protons, neutrons, and electrons. The protons and neutrons are packed inside an extremely tiny region at the center of the atom, called the nucleus. To get an idea of how small the nucleus is, imagine this: If a hydrogen atom were about 4 miles (6.4 kilometers) wide, its nucleus would be less than the size of a tennis ball. Outside the nucleus, the rest of the atom is mostly empty space. This is where the electrons are. They zoom through the empty space at amazing speeds, traveling around the nucleus billions of times in each millionth of a second.

The inner structure of an atom is often compared to the solar system, in which the nucleus represents the Sun and the electrons represent the planets that orbit the Sun. This comparison is not exactly accurate. Earth and the other planets in our solar system follow paths shaped like an ellipse (an oval). The paths of electrons around the nucleus are more complex than that. For example, some electrons travel in spherical orbitals, while others are in dumbbell-shaped orbitals.

More Tiny Particles

In the first twenty-five years of the twentieth century, scientists began to study cosmic rays. Cosmic rays are high-energy particles from outer space that can be detected on mountaintops, where the air is thinner than at sea level. When these rays strike atoms of lead, they knock out a spray of subatomic particles, which are even smaller than protons, neutrons, or electrons. Scientists concluded that these tiny particles were also part of atoms in addition to protons, neutrons, and electrons.

Starting in the 1930s, scientists learned to make particle accelerators. These machines can speed up a particle, such as an electron, to very high speeds. As the particle's speed increases, so does its energy. Scientists use these high-energy particles like bowling balls to hit atoms and knock out particles that can be observed and measured. The use of particle accelerators (sometimes called atom smashers) revealed a number of different kinds of particles hidden inside atoms. In addition to protons, neutrons, and electrons, atoms contain subatomic particles called neutrinos, quarks, and bosons. Scientists of the twenty-first century still use particle accelerators to learn more about the universe. In fact, the world's largest particle accelerator was completed in Switzerland in 2008.

Parts of an Atom

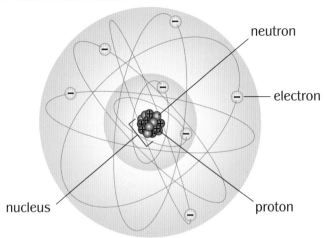

neutron

electron

nucleus

proton

This diagram of the nitrogen atom shows seven tiny electrons whirling around the nucleus. Inside the nucleus are seven protons (red) and seven neutrons (blue). Each proton weighs more than eighteen hundred times as much as an electron.

Just as the planets in our solar system have orbits at different distances from the Sun, the electrons in an atom travel at different distances from the nucleus. (Electrons may be tiny, but they can't all fit into the same place!) They are packed into a series of layers, or electron shells, like the layers of an onion. Each shell can hold only a certain number of electrons. The closest layer to the nucleus holds a maximum of only two electrons, for example, while the next shell can hold eight. The electron shells farther out each have their own limits.

If an atom's outermost electron shell is not exactly full (with the largest number of electrons it can hold), it can react with other atoms. In chemical reactions, an atom may lose electrons or add more electrons—whichever will produce a full outer shell most easily. For example, the metal sodium has three electron shells. Its outer shell contains just a single electron. The gas chlorine has an outer shell that is nearly full, with seven electrons. When these two atoms react, the sodium atom gives the single electron in its outer shell to the chlorine atom. Chlorine now has a full outer shell with eight electrons. Sodium also has a full outer shell, because now its second electron shell—with eight electrons—is the outermost one. (The third shell is empty, so it doesn't count.)

In general, an atom holds the electrons closest to the nucleus most tightly and has the loosest hold on the electrons farthest away from the nucleus. For example, the lithium, sodium, and potassium atoms each have a single electron in their outermost shell. But lithium has only two electron shells, sodium has three, and potassium has four. So lithium holds its single outer electron more tightly than sodium does. A potassium atom holds its outer electron shell even more loosely. As a result, a potassium atom reacts very easily with atoms that can take its extra electron. Sodium gives away its outer electron a little less easily, and lithium even less easily.

Getting a Charge Out of Atoms

When you plug a power cord into an outlet to run a vacuum cleaner, you are using a form of energy called electricity. This kind of energy is an important part of the nature of atoms and the particles they contain.

Sodium Chloride Formation

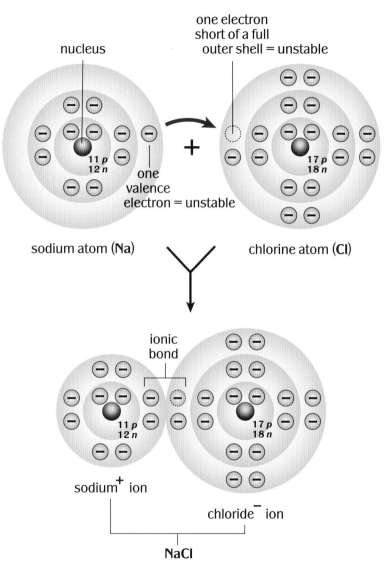

When a sodium atom gives an electron to a chlorine atom, the oppositely charged ions that are formed are attracted to each other. They form a strong ionic bond that holds them together tightly.

How Atoms Become Ions

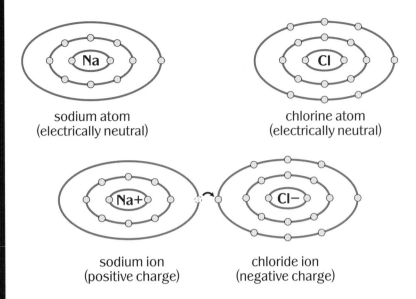

sodium atom
(electrically neutral)

chlorine atom
(electrically neutral)

sodium ion
(positive charge)

chloride ion
(negative charge)

A sodium atom can give an electron to a chlorine atom, leaving each of them with a filled outer electron shell. The atoms have now become electrically charged ions.

Protons carry a positive electric charge, neutrons have no charge, and electrons have a negative charge. Normally, the number of protons in an atom is exactly the same as the number of electrons. Therefore, their charges cancel each other out, and the atom as a whole remains electrically neutral. But an atom can gain or lose electrons in a chemical reaction.

If an atom gains some electrons, it becomes negatively charged. If an atom loses some electrons, it becomes positively charged. Atoms that have an electric charge—either positive or negative—are called ions.

For example, when sodium atoms react with chlorine atoms, they become sodium and chloride ions. The combination of a sodium ion and a chloride ion is called sodium chloride (NaCl), or table salt. The positive charge of the sodium ion (Na^+) cancels out the negative charge of the chloride ion (Cl^-). Therefore, sodium chloride has no electrical charge and is chemically stable (not reactive).

Every charged particle is surrounded by a space around it, in which the charge produces an effect. This space is called an electric field. The electric field causes charged particles to exert a force against one another, even when they are not physically touching one another. Just like a magnet, ions with unlike charges are attracted to one another and like charges repel one another.

Have you ever combed your hair, especially on a dry day, and found that the strands of hair crackle and stand straight up? When the comb goes through your hair, electrons are transferred from your hair to the comb. Now the comb is negatively charged, and your hair is positively charged. So when you bring the comb close to your hair, strands of hair are attracted to the comb. (This is static electricity.)

Static electricity that happens when you brush or comb your hair is caused by the exchange of positive and negative ions.

Forming Molecules

Atoms often join together, or bond, with other atoms to form molecules. A molecule is the basic unit of a substance—the smallest amount that still has the same properties of the substance as a whole.

Each kind of molecule is made up of a different arrangement of atoms to form a unique substance. This grouping of two or more different atoms (a molecule) is called a compound. A compound is a different substance from its ingredients (the atoms). Think about a loaf of bread, for example. The bread is made from flour, yeast, sugar, and water. After you mix the ingredients and bake the dough, you have a new substance—bread. You cannot separate out the flour, yeast, sugar, or water. It's all bread. But chemically, bread is not a single compound. It contains a number of different compounds.

Water, on the other hand, *is* a chemical compound. Every molecule of water consists of exactly two atoms of hydrogen linked to one atom of oxygen. Scientists often refer to water as H_2O (the *H* stands for "hydrogen" and the *O*

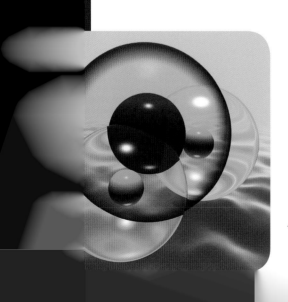

A computer-generated model of a water molecule shows how an oxygen atom (red) and two hydrogen atoms (green) link to form H_2O.

stands for "oxygen"). A single drop of water contains billions of water molecules with billions of hydrogen and oxygen atoms, but it is still called H_2O to indicate that this is its basic unit.

In a mixture, molecules can exist with other molecules, but they do not produce a new, different substance as they do in a compound (such as the bread example above). For example, a tossed salad is a mixture. Unlike the ingredients in bread, the ingredients in a salad—lettuce, carrots, cucumbers, and tomatoes—can be easily separated. The air you breathe is a mixture too—a mixture of gases. It is made up of nitrogen (N_2), oxygen (O_2), and carbon dioxide (CO_2). It also includes water vapor, which can be separated from the air when it condenses into rain or dew.

When water vapor cools, it condenses from a gas state into a liquid state. When water vapor in the air cools overnight, it can become liquid water in the form of dew.

Sticking Together

When two or more atoms join together to form a molecule, what holds them together? Scientists have discovered several main kinds of chemical bonds that hold atoms and molecules together.

These bonds are the main difference between mixtures and compounds. Chemical bonds hold atoms and molecules together so tightly that physical forces cannot separate them. The main types of chemical bonds are ionic bonds, covalent bonds, and polar covalent bonds.

Ionic bonds. This kind of bond is created by the attraction between ions with positive and negative charges. What happens, for example, when a sodium atom joins with a chlorine atom to make sodium chloride (salt)? Does the sodium atom just give an electron away and then never have anything to do with it again? Does the chlorine atom take the extra electron it received from the sodium atom and fly away with it? Actually, no. The sodium and chlorine atoms still stick rather close together after they have become electrically charged sodium and chloride ions. That is because they now have opposite charges—and opposites attract.

The sodium ion is positive because it has given away one of its electrons. Therefore, its total number of protons is one more than the total number of electrons moving around its nucleus. In other words, sodium ions have a charge of +1 (plus one). A chloride ion has received one extra electron. Therefore, its electrons total one more than its protons. It has a charge of −1 (minus one). The attraction between their opposite charges binds them together in an ionic bond.

Ionic bonds are usually quite strong. For example, the salt molecule, sodium chloride, is very stable. This compound is a solid that does not melt until the temperature is very high—1,474°F (801°C). Even more heat or other extreme conditions are needed to break salt down into the atoms that formed it—sodium and chlorine.

Covalent bonds. Not all the chemical bonds that help form molecules are ionic. Some atoms tend to share electrons with other atoms, rather than giving or taking them away. Two atoms of oxygen, for example, can share electrons to form a molecule of oxygen gas—O_2. This kind of bond, in which both atoms still "own" a share of the electrons, is called a covalent bond.

Carbon is a major part of all living things. A carbon atom has four electrons in its outermost shell. It can complete this shell by sharing four electrons with other atoms, forming covalent bonds. For example, carbon can combine with either one or two oxygen atoms, producing carbon monoxide (CO) or carbon dioxide (CO_2). Carbon monoxide is a gas in the exhausts from cars and furnaces. It can be dangerous to breathe if it builds up in a small, closed space. Carbon dioxide is the gas formed when a log of wood burns up in a fire. It is also in the air you exhale.

Carbon atoms can also form covalent bonds with other carbon atoms, forming chains, rings, and complicated branched structures that look like Tinkertoys. These carbon-based molecules build proteins, sugars, fats, and other chemicals that make up living things.

Polar covalent bonds. These chemical bonds are in between covalent and ionic bonds. In a polar covalent bond, atoms are sharing electrons, but one partner in the bond gets a bigger share than the other. In a water molecule, for example, one oxygen atom shares electrons with two hydrogen atoms (H_2O). This forms a molecule that is shaped like a boomerang. Hydrogen is a very tiny atom, with just one proton in its nucleus. Oxygen is a bigger atom. Its nucleus has eight protons. Guess who would win the shared electrons in a tug-of-war between oxygen and hydrogen?

In the water molecule, oxygen does not succeed in pulling the electrons completely away from the two hydrogens bonded to it. Although a hydrogen atom has only one proton, it is *very* close to its electron and has a strong pull on it. But the oxygen has more pulling power. And so the oxygen end of the "boomerang" has a slightly negative charge, and the hydrogen ends are slightly positive. This kind of covalent bond is called a polar covalent bond. (Like a magnet, the molecule has a positive pole and a negative pole.)

The polar covalent bond of water has some special effects on other chemicals. When an ionic compound such as salt is mixed with water, for example, polar water molecules slip in between the ions and separate them. Such mixtures are called solutions. A solution of salt in water will not settle out to form separate solid and liquid layers, no matter how long you leave it.

By keeping ionic compounds in solution, the polar water molecules help them to react with other substances. In fact, most of the reactions in your own body take place in water-based solutions. Water acts like a matchmaker, bringing chemicals together so that reactions between them can occur.

Is It a Mixture or a Solution?

A mixture is a combination of two or more different substances. It can be separated by physical means. For example, if you mixed sugar and salt crystals, you could then use a magnifying lens and tweezers to separate the two kinds of crystals. If a muddy mixture of soil and water is allowed to stand, the solid soil particles will gradually settle to the bottom, leaving a clear layer of water on top. In both cases, the mixtures can be separated without changing them chemically.

Solutions are one type of mixture. They normally cannot be separated without changing the chemicals that formed them. Both salt and sugar, for example, dissolve in water and form solutions. No matter how long you allow these solutions to stand, they will stay unchanged. But you can boil off the water (changing its state from liquid to gas), leaving only the solid salt or sugar behind.

The ancient Greeks believed that all matter is made up of varying amounts of four basic building blocks, or elements: earth, water, air, and fire. That may seem amusing in modern times, when scientists have discovered and named more than one hundred elements. But the idea of matter consisting of only four elements was generally accepted in the Western world for about two thousand years.

Discovering Elements

An element is a substance made up of only one type of atom. Not everyone agrees about who discovered the elements. Take the element hydrogen, for example. In the sixteenth century, a Swiss scientist named Paracelsus produced hydrogen gas when he mixed iron with a strong acid, sulfuric acid. But he didn't know what it was. He described the gas as "an air which bursts forth like the wind."

More than a century later, in the 1650s, English scientist Robert Boyle also dissolved iron in an acid. He called the gas that formed the "inflammable solution of iron" because it burst into flames when it came in contact with air. Boyle also discovered that water was formed in this explosive reaction.

Modern historians of science, however, credit the discovery of hydrogen to a different English scientist, Henry Cavendish. In 1766 Cavendish produced hydrogen by dropping pieces of several different metals into acid solutions. He called this gas "inflammable air from the metals." Cavendish was the first scientist to investigate the properties of this "inflammable air." He found that it is lighter than any other substance. He also studied its reaction with air and worked out how much of each gas took part in the reaction. He didn't realize that only part of the air reacted (the oxygen), but he did establish that water was not an element. It was a compound formed from two separate gases. (Hydrogen was finally named about twenty years later by French scientist Antoine Lavoisier. He created the name from two Greek words meaning "water former.")

The element oxygen was discovered by an English minister, Joseph Priestley. His hobby was science. He ran a series of experiments studying various kinds of gases. When

Priestley placed a lighted candle in a sealed container of ordinary air, the candle burned for a while and then went out. If he placed a living plant in the same container, the candle went on burning.

In 1774 Priestley used a magnifying glass to focus sunlight on a lump of mercury compound. This reaction formed a gas (oxygen), which was captured in an upside-down glass container, sealed at the bottom. Priestley found that a lighted candle, placed in this gas-filled container, burned much more brightly than usual. He also tried breathing the gas he had made and was able to breathe more easily than with ordinary air. (Modern doctors sometimes give patients with lung diseases pure oxygen to breathe through a tube or mask.)

Just three years later, French scientist Lavoisier solved another great mystery of science when he discovered what fire really is. In a paper published in 1777, he explained that burning is a chemical

French scientist Antoine Lavoisier made discoveries about oxygen that helped later scientists understand how atoms work together.

reaction in which oxygen combines with a substance such as charcoal or hydrogen. He demonstrated that oxygen is a part of air and gave oxygen its name, which means "acid former." (Lavoisier had burned phosphorus and sulfur, producing phosphoric and sulfuric acids.) In other experiments, Lavoisier demonstrated that oxygen is involved not only in burning but also in the rusting of iron and the respiration (breathing) of living creatures.

The discoveries of the late 1700s led the way to the development of atomic theory—the basis of all modern chemistry. John Dalton, an English chemist, created atomic theory in 1808. He explained that everything on Earth is made of a certain number of basic elements, such as hydrogen, oxygen, carbon, and lead. Each element is made of just one kind of atom, and each compound is formed by a certain combination of atoms. Remember water is made up of one atom of oxygen and two atoms of hydrogen (H_2O). But if you combine an atom of oxygen with an atom of

Did You Know?

Antoine Lavoisier worked up a list of more than thirty elements, including oxygen, hydrogen, nitrogen, phosphorus, sulfur, mercury, and zinc. He mistakenly thought that light and heat were elements too. In fact, light is a visible form of radiation, while heat is a form of energy produced by the random movement of molecules. Neither is a form of matter, much less one of its basic building blocks.

English chemist John Dalton created the atomic theory of matter. He discovered that atoms of different elements combine in specific amounts to form compounds.

carbon, the result is carbon monoxide (CO). If you take two atoms of oxygen and combine them with one carbon atom, you produce carbon dioxide (CO_2). Therefore, these chemical compounds are created from combinations of a few basic atoms.

Dalton also showed that each element has its own atomic weight—that is, the total number of protons and neutrons in an atom's nucleus. The number of protons in an atom's nucleus is called the atomic number. (The number of protons is the same as the number of electrons in an atom.) For example, the lightest element, hydrogen, has only one proton and no neutrons. Therefore, hydrogen's atomic number and atomic weight are both 1. Oxygen has eight protons and eight neutrons. Therefore, its atomic number is 8 and its atomic weight is 16.

Three of a Kind

Although the atoms of an element all share the same chemical properties, they may have different weights. Most hydrogen nuclei, for example, contain one proton and no neutrons. But some hydrogen nuclei do have one neutron. This form of hydrogen has an atomic weight of 2. Hydrogen atoms with these heavier nuclei are called heavy hydrogen, or deuterium. (Those with just a proton are called protium.)

A third variety of hydrogen atoms exists too, and it is far rarer and even heavier. It is called tritium. Each of its nuclei contains one proton and two neutrons, for an atomic weight of 3. These various forms of hydrogen—protium, deuterium, and tritium—are called isotopes of hydrogen. Isotopes of an element all have the same atomic number (1 in the case of hydrogen) but different atomic weights.

Most elements have at least one isotope in addition to the most common (less heavy) form. Uranium, one of the heaviest elements, has fourteen isotopes. Each uranium isotope has an atomic number of 92 (that is, it has 92 protons). The heaviest uranium isotope, U-238, has 146 neutrons. Combined with its 92 protons, the atomic weight of this uranium isotope is 238.

Sorting the Elements

By the mid-1800s, Russian chemist Dmitri Ivanovitch Mendeleev figured out how to sort the chemical elements into a system, which is known as the periodic table of the elements. Mendeleev was an avid card-player, and the game of solitaire inspired his element-sorting system. In solitaire the cards are organized first horizontally and then vertically by suit and then by number. Mendeleev decided to write down the names of all of the elements known at the time, along with their atomic weights, on blank cards. He laid the cards out like a solitaire deck, in order of increasing atomic

Russian chemist Dmitri Mendeleev invented the periodic table of elements by arranging the known elements in columns and rows according to their atomic weights. This led to many insights about their behavior in chemical reactions.

weight. It was then that he found a pattern.

He noticed that elements with similar properties and reactions seemed to occur regularly. Sodium and potassium, for example, are both metals and both combine with chlorine to form a salt. Their salts are so similar that, in modern times, potassium chloride is sold as a salt substitute for people on a low-sodium diet.

Mendeleev then sorted these "families" of elements into the first periodic table of elements. He arranged them vertically into columns (called groups) and horizontally in rows (called periods). There were some gaps, but Mendeleev predicted that three elements yet to be discovered would fill those gaps. He was right. By the end of the nineteenth century, scientists found the missing elements—gallium, germanium, and scandium. They fit perfectly into his chart.

Scientists use one- or two-letter abbreviations for the names

Did You Know?

The elements in the modern periodic table are arranged according to their atomic number, rather than atomic weight. Hydrogen (H) is the first one listed. It has an atomic number of 1. In modern times, different sources list different *total* numbers of known elements—from 109 up to 118—because scientists keep finding and making new ones. Of the more than one hundred known elements, more than ninety occur naturally on Earth. The rest are made artificially.

Periodic Table of the Elements

Legend		
■ Alkali Metals	■ Alkaline Earth Metals	□ Transition Metals
■ Rare Earth Metals	■ Metalliods	□ Other Metals
□ Nonmetals	■ Halogens	□ Noble Gases

Be 4												B 5	C 6	N 7	O 8	F 9	He 2
Mg 12												Al 13	Si 14	P 15	S 16	Cl 17	Ne 10
Ca 20	Sc 21	Ti 22	V 23	Cr 24	Mn 25	Fe 26	Co 27	Ni 28	Cu 29	Zn 30	Ga 31	Ge 32	As 33	Se 34	Br 35		Ar 18
Sr 38	Y 39	Zr 40	Nb 41	Mo 42	Tc 43	Ru 44	Rh 45	Pd 46	Ag 47	Cd 48	In 49	Sn 50	Sb 51	Te 52	I 53		Kr 36
Ba 56	La-Lu 57-71	Hf 72	Ta 73	W 74	Re 75	Os 76	Ir 77	Pt 78	Au 79	Hg 80	Tl 81	Pb 82	Bi 83	Po 84	At 85		Xe 54
Ra 88	Ac-Lr 89-103	Rf 104	Db 105	Sg 24	Bh 107	Hs 108	Mt 109	Uun 110	Uuu 111	Uub 112		Uuq 114					Rn 86

lanthanides	La 57	Ce 58	Pr 59	Nd 60	Pm 61	Sm 62	Eu 63	Gd 64	Tb 65	Dy 66	Ho 67	Er 68	Tm 69	Yb 70	Lu 71
actinides	Ac 89	Th 90	Pa 91	U 92	Np 93	Pu 94	Am 95	Cm 96	Bk 97	Cf 98	Es 99	Fm 100	Md 101	No 102	Lr 103

Mendeleev's periodic table reveals the similarities and differences of the elements. Metals are on the left, and nonmetals are on the right.

of the elements. C is carbon, for example, N is nitrogen, and Al is aluminum. Usually the symbol for an element is made up of the first letter of its name. When more than one element starts with the same letter, a second letter from its name is used to show which element it refers to. Mg, for example, stands for magnesium, and Mn stands for manganese.

Some of the symbols for the elements are not so obvious. Copper is Cu, sodium is Na, and iron is Fe. Where did those letters come from? They were taken from the Latin names for the elements: *cuprum* for copper, *natrium* for sodium, and *ferrum* for iron. K for potassium comes from the German *kalium*.

Metals vs. Nonmetals

Nearly 80 percent of all the known elements are metals. They are found on the left side of Mendeleev's periodic table. A number of everyday objects are made of metal, such as aluminum pots, copper wire, and iron nails.

Most metal objects, however, are not usually made of *pure* metals. They are made of mixtures of different metals, called alloys. That is because most metals are not very strong in their pure form. They may also rust or stain when they are exposed to air, dust, or dirt. Alloys are harder, stronger, and longer lasting than pure metals. For example, steel, an important alloy, has iron as its main ingredient. Steel is used in products such as cars, buildings, and knife blades. Brass, bronze, and sterling silver are other examples of alloys.

Nearly all metals are solids, with high melting and boiling points. Most metals are chemically reactive. They are more likely to be found combined with other elements, such as oxygen, sulfur, and chlorine. Metals can be worked into different shapes by hammering them, and they can be drawn out into long, thin wires. Metals are good conductors—they can transfer heat and electricity easily.

Like other metal elements, copper is a good conductor of electricity.

Matter through the Ages

The earliest part of human history on Earth is known as the Stone Age. Early humans made tools by chipping stones to make a sharp, cutting edge. Much later, people learned to work metals and learned to make alloys by blending metals together. These discoveries led to huge advancements in tool making. The period of human history from about 3500 to 1000 B.C. is called the Bronze Age. Many useful tools were made from bronze, an alloy of copper and tin that is harder and stronger than either of those elements alone.

After that came the Iron Age, which began around 1000 B.C. and lasted several thousand years. People learned to get metallic iron out of the rocks containing iron compounds. Tools and weapons made of iron and its alloys were stronger and more useful than those made of bronze. The modern world has been called the Silicon Age, because we depend so much on computers that work on tiny chips of the element silicon.

That is why a pot on the stove quickly gets hot all over when the heat is turned on under it. Metal wires conduct electricity from outlets in the wall to lamps and appliances throughout a house. The wires are usually covered with plastic or some other nonconducting material (insulation) to keep people from getting a shock.

The right side of Mendeleev's periodic table contains the nonmetals. Although there are far more kinds of metals than nonmetals, the nonmetals actually account for more of Earth's matter. Many of the nonmetals are gases, but some are solids.

Earth's atmosphere is made up mainly of two gases—nitrogen and oxygen. The rocks that form Earth's crust are combinations of metals with nonmetals such as oxygen, sulfur, nitrogen, and chlorine. Roughly two-thirds of our planet is covered with water, which is a combination of two nonmetals—hydrogen and oxygen. In general, nonmetals do not conduct heat and electricity.

Has anyone told you that you look just like one of your parents or maybe a grandparent or an aunt or uncle? Family members have many traits in common. They may not only look alike, with a similar shape of the nose or ears, eye color, and height—they may also have a similar way or walking or talking or the same sense of humor. But there are also individual differences, even among brothers and sisters.

Like people, the chemical elements have general family similarities and individual differences. The main characteristic that chemical family members share is their chemical behavior—how they react with other chemicals. Let's take a closer look at a number of common elements and the families to which they belong.

Hydrogen

At the top left corner of the periodic table, hydrogen stands all alone. It is the smallest and lightest of all the atoms, with nothing else like it. With a single electron in its outer (only) shell, it is very reactive.

In fact, it does not exist naturally in the form of single atoms. Hydrogen gas is made up of H_2 molecules, in which two hydrogen atoms share their electrons.

Hydrogen can also give away an electron, producing a hydrogen ion (H^{+1}) with a positive charge. It can also accept an electron from a metal, forming a negatively charged hydride ion (H^{-1}), or share electrons with other atoms, such as oxygen. Hydrogen burns when exposed to air, which means that it makes a good fuel. But it must be protected from air when pure hydrogen gas is stored and used.

Normally hydrogen is not found on Earth in pure form, except in gas-filled pockets trapped in rocks underground. But it is the most abundant element in the universe. The Sun and other stars are made mostly of hydrogen.

The Alkali Metals

Directly below hydrogen in the periodic table is a group of elements that also have a single electron in their outer shell. These are all metals that belong to a family called the alkali metals. They can donate their outermost electron to form stable salts with ionic (electrically charged) bonds.

This section of the periodic table of elements shows hydrogen along with the alkali metals.

The lightest alkali metal is lithium, with an atomic number of 3 and an atomic weight of nearly 7, corresponding to three protons and four neutrons. (This element actually has two isotopes, with atomic weights of 6 and 7. About 92 percent of the lithium found in nature is lithium-7.) Lithium is a soft, light, silvery white metal. The pure metal is not found in nature. It usually exists in the form of various minerals (compounds found in rocks), such as lithium carbonate. Lithium compounds are used in long-life batteries and also in making glasses, ceramics, rubbers, and dyes. Lithium carbonate is sometimes used as a drug to treat a form of mental illness called bipolar disorder.

Sodium, the next in the alkali group, is a gray solid, which is as soft as butter. It can be cut with a

Sodium is an alkali metal. It is a soft, silver metal that reacts quickly with water and oxygen.

knife or molded easily, but it is so reactive that it will burn you if you touch it with your bare hand. When freshly cut, sodium is shiny, but its surface quickly turns dull because it reacts immediately with oxygen in the air.

Sodium reacts with water, forming sodium hydroxide (NaOH) and releasing hydrogen. The reaction is so violent that the hydrogen may explode! Another name for sodium hydroxide is lye, which is found in some drain cleaners. It is also used in refining petroleum and in making paper, soaps, and textiles. Other sodium compounds include sodium bicarbonate (baking soda), which helps dough rise and can calm an upset stomach, and sodium nitrate, which is used as a fertilizer. Various other sodium compounds are used in industry, medicine, and photography.

Too Much of a Good Thing?

Do you use the saltshaker at every meal? Many people do. Common table salt makes food taste better. It is an important chemical in the body, helping to make muscles contract and to send messages along nerves. But medical experts say that we eat too much salt—that the foods in a balanced diet naturally supply all the salt we need, without adding any from a saltshaker. For many people, eating too much salt can lead to high blood pressure, which increases the risk of having a heart attack or a stroke.

The rest of the alkali group includes potassium, rubidium, cesium, and francium. They are silver-colored metals that react chemically very much like sodium. Potassium reacts so readily with water and air that it occurs naturally only in minerals, in which it is combined with other elements. Rubidium is a radioactive element that is formed in nuclear reactions.

What Is Radioactivity?

The nuclei of some atoms, especially the largest ones, are unstable. Over time, they tend to decay or break apart into smaller groups of particles. Even stable isotopes can be broken apart by an outside energy source. And nuclei can be forced to join together under certain conditions. These reactions of the nucleus are called nuclear reactions.

Scientists of the late 1800s noticed that after a nuclear reaction occurs, the weight of the newly formed particles seems to be a bit less than it was at the start of the process. But how could weight suddenly disappear? In 1905 scientist Albert Einstein proved that a tiny amount of mass can be converted into a large amount of energy. Every nuclear reaction

The Alkaline Earth Metals

This group of elements is just to the right of the alkali metals in the periodic table. They all have two electrons in their outermost shell and can donate them to other elements in forming ionic bonds.

Beryllium is a brittle, light gray metal. It is rather rare and is found only in minerals such as beryl. Emeralds are a form of beryl crystals with a dark green color.

---

involves a conversion of mass to energy, which is why particles weigh less after a nuclear reaction.

Radioactivity is a type of nuclear reaction. The nucleus of a radioactive atom breaks down and changes into another kind of element or isotope. As it forms a new nucleus or splits into two or more new nuclei, it releases radiation. Scientists measure the rate of radioactive decay (breakdown) in units of time called half-lives. This is the amount of time it takes for half of the atoms of a particular radioisotope to decay into another element or isotope. The heavier the atom, the longer it takes to decay. Tritium, the heaviest form of hydrogen, is a radioactive isotope with a half-life of about twelve years. Uranium-238 is a much heavier radioisotope that takes a much longer time to decay—its half-life is about five billion years.

Be
BERYLLIUM
4

Mg
MAGNESIUM
12

Ca
CALCIUM
20

Sr
STRONTIUM
38

Ba
BARIUM
56

Ra
RADIUM
88

This portion of the periodic table shows the alkaline earth metals—metals that can form chemical bonds by giving away two electrons.

Magnesium is a silver white metal that is light but strong. It is abundant in the rocks of Earth's crust, in the form of minerals, and also makes up about 0.13 percent of seawater. This element plays important roles in living things. It is part of chlorophyll, a compound used by plants when they make food by the light-sensitive process in nature called photosynthesis. It also helps out in many chemical reactions in the bodies of animals.

Magnesium is very reactive. Strips of this metal are used to protect steel pipes and water tanks from the destructive action of water and soil chemicals. Magnesium is also used as a construction material for aircraft and automobile parts, where a combination of lightness and strength is important. Fertilizers containing magnesium provide an important raw material for chlorophyll, the energy-absorbing pigment that gives plants their green color. This element is also used for its calming qualities in common medicines such as milk of magnesia and Epsom salts.

Calcium is a soft, silvery white metal found in rocks such as limestone and marble. It is one of the most abundant metals, found in about 3.5 percent of Earth's crust. In humans and other animals, calcium is needed to build strong bones and teeth. It also takes part in many important reactions in the body, helping blood to clot and muscles to contract. Milk and other dairy products are good food sources of calcium.

Strontium, the next alkaline earth metal, is chemically very similar to calcium. This element caused problems when the United States, Soviet Union, and other nations started testing nuclear weapons in the 1950s and 1960s. When such weapons explode, one of the isotopes of strontium, strontium-90, is

During a nuclear reaction, a radioactive form of strontium enters the atmosphere and is very poisonous.

formed. It can enter the atmosphere and be carried all over the world by the winds. This isotope is highly radioactive and is very poisonous to living things. When strontium-90 falls to the ground, it is taken up by plants and then by the animals that eat them. It can also contaminate water supplies.

In the body, part of the strontium-90 is deposited in bones in place of calcium. There it stays for the rest of a person's life, sending out tiny bursts of radiation that can damage body tissues and lead to cancer and other illnesses. Nuclear weapons are no longer tested in the open atmosphere. But hundreds of nuclear power plants around the world rely on contained nuclear reactions to generate electricity. Although the power plants have strict safety rules, accidents can happen. In 1986, for example, the nuclear power plant in Chernobyl in Ukraine exploded and sprayed strontium-90 fallout over nearby areas. Thousands of people died or fell ill, and the cleanup took three years.

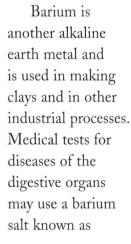

Barium is another alkaline earth metal and is used in making clays and in other industrial processes. Medical tests for diseases of the digestive organs may use a barium salt known as

This photo shows the Chernobyl nuclear power plant after the 1986 explosion.

barium sulfate. The person drinks a mixture of the barium salt in water. It coats the insides of the esophagus, stomach, and intestines as it makes its way out of the body. Doctors can then review the outline of the organs, as highlighted by the barium sulfate in X-ray pictures.

Radium, the heaviest of the alkaline earths, is radioactive. It is formed in deposits of uranium minerals as the isotope U-238 decays. The radium breaks down in turn, forming a gas called radon.

The Transition Metals

To the right of the alkaline earth metals in the periodic table is a sort of wide bridge of elements in the lower part of the table. These are the transition metals. They give away electrons to form ionic bonds. They do not always give away the same number of electrons for a particular element, however. Iron, for example,

If She Had Only Known!

Marie Curie, a French physicist, discovered radium in 1898 and much of her research dealt with radioactive materials. She won two Nobel Prizes for her work, but at the time, no one realized how dangerous radioactivity can be. Marie Curie died of leukemia, a disease in which white blood cells multiply uncontrollably. Medical historians believe her condition was most likely caused by her many exposures to radioactive materials over a long period of time.

	Ti TITANIUM 22	V VANADIUM 23	Cr CHROMIUM 24	Mn MANGANESE 25	Fe IRON 26	Co COBALT 27	Ni NICKEL 28	Cu COPPER 29	Zn ZINC 30
	Zr ZIRCONIUM 40	Nb NIOBIUM 41	Mo MOLYBDENUM 42	Tc TECHNETIUM 43	Ru RUTHENIUM 44	Rh RHODIUM 45	Pd PALLADIUM 46	Ag SILVER 47	Cd CADMIUM 48
	Hf HAFNIUM 72	Ta TANTALUM 73	W TUNGSTEN 74	Re RHENIUM 75	Os OSMIUM 76	Ir IRIDIUM 77	Pt PLATINUM 78	Au GOLD 79	Hg MERCURY 80
	Rf RUTHERFORDIUM 104	Db DUBNIUM 105	Sg SEABORGIUM 24	Bh BOHRIUM 107	Hs HASSIUM 108	Mt MEITNERIUM 109	Uun UNUNNILIUM 110	Uuu UNUNUNIUM 111	Uub UNUNBIUM 112

The transition metals can vary in the number of electrons they give away. The lanthanides (57–71) and actinides (89–103) are two series of "rare earth metals."

can donate either two or three electrons, and copper usually donates one or two. This happens because these elements can shuffle their electrons between the two electron shells farthest out from the nucleus.

The transition metal group includes many familiar metals that are used in the form of pure metals and alloys as building materials, machine parts, and decorative objects. Iron, nickel, chromium, zinc, and lead all belong to this group. So do the precious metals, such as silver, gold, and platinum. (They are called precious because they are both rare and beautiful.) Mercury, the only metal that is liquid at room temperature, is also a transition metal.

The Other Metals

The right side of the periodic table is not as neat and simple as the left. Instead of straight vertical

Do You Have Mercury in Your Teeth?

Mercury readily joins with silver and other metals to form alloys called amalgams. When heated, they are soft enough to be molded into shape, but then they cool down into a very strong, hard material that has long been used to fill cavities in people's teeth.

Some forms of mercury are very poisonous and can cause serious nerve and muscle diseases and even death. These forms of mercury can dissolve in water and then can pass through the body fluids into the tissues and organs. Many medical experts believe that amalgams used by dentists do not do this—they just sit there in a person's teeth without interacting with the body tissues. Some experts, however, believe that tiny amounts of active mercury—enough to cause trouble—may leak out of fillings. This question is still very controversial, but some people have had their amalgam fillings removed and replaced by plastic mixtures that do not contain metals.

columns, some of the groups of related elements form triangles and diagonals. The first is a group of metals headed by aluminum. It is a light but strong metal that is the most abundant of all the metals on Earth. In fact, aluminum is the third most abundant element in Earth's crust, after oxygen and silicon. Aluminum is widely used as a building material, in food containers, pots and pans, and foil wrappers. In chemical reactions, aluminum tends to donate three electrons to form salts. It can also share electrons with elements such as oxygen.

Tin is another metal in this group. Its chemical symbol is Sn, which comes from its Latin name, *stannum*. Tin cans actually are made of steel, with a thin coating of tin. This shiny metal protects the steel from rusting. Protective tin coatings are also used on paper clips, safety pins, straight pins, and staples. Tin is used in the alloys bronze and pewter.

Another important member of this group is lead. This metal is very heavy, but it has a lower melting point than most other metals and is rather soft. One problem with the wide use of lead is that it is poisonous. If it gets into the body, this metal can build up over time and cause a lot of damage. The effects of lead poisoning may include weakened bones and muscles, brain damage, deafness, and speech problems. Before 1978 lead was used in homes for water pipes and tanks and in paints. It is no longer used for these purposes in the United States, but young children who eat peeling paint or contaminated dust or soil from around windowsills and moldings of old houses can still get lead poisoning. (Lead paints have a sweet taste.) The paints used on children's toys made in developing countries such as China can also be dangerous for young children.

Cars made from the mid-1940s to the late 1970s ran on a type of gasoline to which a lead compound was added to help it burn more smoothly. But scientists found that lead was released in the car exhaust gases. It got into the air and contaminated food and water. In the United States and many other countries, starting in the mid-1970s, the use of "leaded" gasoline was gradually stopped. It is still being used in developing countries, however.

The Metalloids

This is a small group of in-between elements, on a diagonal between the metals and the nonmetals. The elements include boron, silicon, germanium, arsenic,

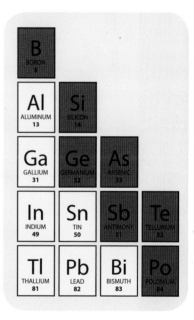

The "other metals" and "metalloids" are groups of in-between elements, which are similar to metals in some ways but act like nonmetals in others.

antimony, tellurium, and polonium. These seven elements are called metall*oids* because in some ways they act like metals, but in others, they are more like nonmetals. The metalloids are semiconductors. They carry electricity at high temperatures, but at low temperatures, they are nonconductors, or insulators. Semiconductors such as silicon and germanium are very important in the modern world. They form the basis of the chips used in building computers.

Silicon Life?

Life on Earth is based on carbon compounds. Silicon is not as abundant on our planet as carbon, but chemically it is similar to carbon. Like carbon, silicon can form covalent bonds by sharing the four electrons in its outer shell with other atoms. For example, the sand on a beach is made up of silicon dioxide (SiO_2). More complicated silicon compounds form plastics and are used in plastic surgery.

Could silicon compounds be the basis of different forms of life on other planets? Some scientists have suggested that it could. These alien life-forms would probably be stonelike beings, like animated crystals. Their brains might be like the silicon chips in computers.

Nonmetals

Some very important elements form a small triangle above and to the right of the metalloid group in the periodic table. Carbon, nitrogen, and oxygen are in the top row. Below them are phosphorus and sulfur in the second row and selenium in the third row.

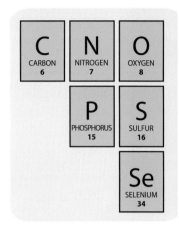

These six nonmetals tend to share electrons when they form compounds. They are all important elements in living organisms.

The element carbon is a solid that can occur in several different forms, including diamond (sparkling crystals), graphite (a greasy gray or black solid used as a lubricant), and charcoal (the crumbly black powder that remains after wood is burned). Carbon is found in all the living things on Earth. It can share its outer four electrons with a variety of other elements. (It therefore forms covalent bonds, not ionic bonds.) Carbon compounds can be as simple as carbon monoxide (CO) and methane (CH_4). But many of the carbon compounds in living organisms (biochemicals) are very complex, containing thousands of atoms joined in chains, rings, and three-dimensional shapes.

Did You Know?

Carbon makes up only 0.8 percent of Earth's crust but makes up about 18 percent of the human body.

Buckyballs

Under special conditions, groups of sixty carbon atoms can form solid structures that look like tiny soccer balls. The carbon atoms are arranged much like the interlocking hexagons and pentagons of a geodesic dome. This unusual structure was developed in the mid-1900s by architect R. Buckminster Fuller, so the tiny carbon balls were named buckminsterfullerene, or buckyballs *(left)*.

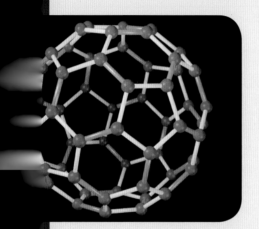

Buckyballs are hollow, and various elements can be trapped inside or substituted for one or more of the carbon atoms. Buckyballs can also be built into tiny tubes, called nanotubes. (*Nano* meanas "one-billionth.") Buckyball products can be used to build tiny machines, too small to see without a microscope. Nanomachines may someday do medical jobs inside the body, such as repairing damaged blood vessels or measuring the amount of sugar in the blood.

Nitrogen is a gas that makes up about four-fifths of Earth's atmosphere. The element occurs as a combination of two nitrogen atoms (N_2) and is not very reactive. Nitrogen can also be a part of salts such as nitrates, nitrites, and nitrides, in which it shares its electrons in various ways. Soil bacteria take nitrogen out of the air and change it into nitrogen salts. Bacteria that live in special nodules (swellings) on the roots of plants such as peas, beans, and alfalfa also help in making nitrogen from the air available to plants and to animals that eat them.

About one-fifth of Earth's atmosphere is oxygen. Like nitrogen, this gas occurs in the form of two atoms joined together (O_2). Oxygen is absolutely vital to almost all the living things on Earth. Their body cells combine oxygen with food materials to generate energy, in a process somewhat like the burning of a fire. (In a fire, oxygen combines with burnable materials such as wood or paper. In living organisms, however, the reaction occurs in such small amounts that it does not produce flames.)

Three oxygen atoms can join together, forming ozone (O_3). Some ozone is found in the air we breathe, especially when air pollution is high. Ozone is rather unstable and can cause damage if it gets into the body. It irritates the lungs and can bring on asthma attacks and other breathing problems.

Most of the elements in this group play important roles in the chemistry of living organisms. Oxygen is a major part of starches, sugars, fats, and various other biochemicals. Nitrogen is a key part of proteins, and it is also found in other compounds, such as some hormones and vitamins. Phosphates (combinations of phosphorus and oxygen) form the framework of deoxyribonucleic acid, or DNA (the chemical that contains the hereditary information in cells). Sulfur is also found in food and body chemicals, especially smelly ones, such as garlic, cabbage, and body wastes.

Selenium compounds occur in minerals in Earth's crust. Plants take in selenium from the soil, and animals get it by eating plant products. In our bodies, this nonmetal is a part of some important enzymes

Where Did the Ozone Go?

We usually think of ozone in the air as a bad thing. But ozone in the upper atmosphere actually protects us and other living organisms from damaging effects of the Sun. This ozone is formed when ultraviolet (UV) rays from the Sun hit oxygen molecules. The ozone acts as a shield, preventing harmful radiations from reaching Earth's surface. In the late 1970s, however, scientists found that there was a hole in the ozone layer over the Antarctic—and the hole was getting bigger. If this loss continued, going out on a sunny day could result in skin cancer, cataracts (clouding of the eye lens), and other harmful effects.

(chemicals that help chemical reactions take place). In large amounts, though, selenium is poisonous.

The Halogen Group

This group of nonmetals can be found in the second column from the right side of the periodic table. The members of this group are fluorine, chlorine, bromine, iodine, and astatine. Fluorine and chlorine exist as gases at room temperature. Each is so reactive that single atoms are not stable. Like oxygen and nitrogen, they combine with another atom to make F_2 and Cl_2. Bromine is a liquid, and both iodine and astatine are solids.

Where had the ozone gone? It turned out that compounds of halogens with carbon, called CFCs (chlorofluorocarbons), were the reason. These compounds were being used in refrigerators and air conditioners and also in aerosol spray cans. They were escaping into the air and rising to the upper atmosphere, where they reacted with the ozone layer.

In 1989 the United States and about two dozen other nations began to replace CFCs with HFCs (hydrofluorocarbons), which do not harm the ozone layer. Other nations joined in, and by 1998, 160 countries had agreed to stop making and using CFCs. The size of the ozone hole has been slowly decreasing since then.

The halogens (shown here in the left column) *are the most reactive nonmetals, gaining an electron when they form compounds. The noble gases* (the right column) *don't usually react at all.*

All halogens have seven electrons in their outer shell, which means that they need just one more electron to fill it. They readily bond with metals of the groups on the far left of the periodic table to form salts. (*Halogen* means "salt former.") Remember that common table salt is NaCl (sodium chloride).

Fluorine, the lightest of the halogens, is the most reactive of all the elements in the periodic table. Small amounts of fluoride salts are added to toothpaste and, in some areas, to drinking water. They combine with tooth enamel and strengthen it, helping to prevent tooth decay.

Bleach contains a rather unstable compound of chlorine, which breaks down on contact with air, releasing chlorine atoms. These very reactive atoms change the chemicals in stains on clothing to colorless compounds. Both chlorine and iodine kill germs and are used as disinfectants. Bromine is also used as a disinfectant and is a part of fireproofing chemicals, pesticides, and dyes, as well.

The Noble Gases

The last group, at the far right side of the periodic table, consists of elements that do not react under normal conditions. Their outer shell is already filled with the maximum number of electrons. So they have no need to give away, receive, or share electrons with other elements. The noble gases include helium, neon, argon, krypton, xenon, and radon. All of them occur naturally and are found in very small amounts in the atmosphere.

Helium, the lightest of the noble gases, has only two protons in its nucleus. It is very rare on Earth but rather common in the universe. The Sun and the other stars are made up mainly of hydrogen and helium. Helium is formed in a nuclear reaction when two hydrogen nuclei join, or fuse, together. This fusion reaction generates huge amounts of energy that keeps the Sun burning brightly.

The noble gases are used under conditions when a very stable atmosphere is needed. Argon, for example, is used to fill lightbulbs. It does not catch fire or explode when the electricity heats the tiny wire inside that makes the lightbulb glow.

Brightly colored neon signs are gas-filled tubes through which electricity is passed. Neon gas normally glows reddish orange. Other elements, including argon, mercury, krypton, and xenon, may be added to produce different colors.

Radon is a radioactive gas. It is formed in a nuclear reaction from the element radium. In certain areas, the soil and rocks contain radium minerals. Radon leaks out and may concentrate in basements and other closed-in areas, causing a radiation hazard for people living or working in the building.

Chemical reactions happen around us all the time—

when we light a match, start a car, eat a hamburger,

bake a cake, run around in gym class, and even when

we are sound asleep. A chemical reaction is what

happens when two or more atoms or molecules form

bonds and create brand new substances. When a

sodium atom (Na) bonds with a chlorine atom (Cl), this

is a chemical reaction. It forms the salt you sprinkle on

your food (NaCl).

The water you drink (H_2O) can be formed by many different chemical reactions. The simplest is one you already know about: two atoms of hydrogen join with one atom of oxygen. That's the thing about chemical reactions—they are predictable. Chemical reactions will happen the same way every single time, as long as the conditions are the same. Sodium plus chlorine will always form salt. Hydrogen will always form water when it combines with oxygen.

Scientists use the symbols of the elements as a quick way of showing how reactions occur. Any

Many centuries ago, a group of scientists known as alchemists believed that they could turn metals such as lead into gold. Of course, this was not possible—except, perhaps, by nuclear reactions, which no one knew about at the time. However, the alchemists made many important contributions to science in the process of trying. They invented tools for experimenting, such as bottles and beakers to hold their chemicals, ovens to heat them, and scales to weigh out exact amounts of powders. They also created many useful substances, such as acids and alcohols.

reaction can be written in the form of an equation, in which the reactants (the chemicals that are reacting) are on the left and the products (the substances that are formed) are on the right. Usually an arrow is used in place of an equal sign in the middle, to show which way the reaction is going. For example, this is the equation for the formation of water from hydrogen and oxygen:

$$2H_2 + O_2 \rightarrow 2H_2O$$

Why isn't the equation written simply as $H_2 + O \rightarrow H_2O$? First of all, oxygen, like hydrogen, contains two atoms in its elemental form (O_2). But if we wrote $H_2 + O_2 \rightarrow H_2O$, the two sides of the equation would not be equal. There would be two atoms of oxygen on the left and only one on the right. What actually happens is that the second oxygen atom reacts with *another* hydrogen molecule to form another water molecule, for a total of two water molecules as the product.

Acids and Bases

Acids and bases are everywhere. Not only can they be found in factories and laboratories, you can also find them around your own home. Most of the liquids you see contain ions, and these ions may make the solution either acidic or basic. Pure water is an exception to this rule. It is neither an acid nor a base. It is neutral. But the water that comes out of the faucet in the sink contains various salts and other substances. (Tap water may be neutral, acidic, or basic, depending on what impurities it contains.) Even bottled spring water is not pure.

An acid is a substance that contains hydrogen ions (H^+). Acids are usually sour tasting, and they can dissolve (form a solution) in water. Vinegar is an acid. So are oranges and lemons, which contain an acid called citric acid. (That is what gives lemonade its tangy taste.) Citric acid and the acetic acid in vinegar are weak acids. A car battery contains a very strong type of acid, called sulfuric acid. Strong acids can burn skin and eat through metals.

A base is a substance that produces hydroxyl ions (OH^-). Bases are bitter tasting and can dissolve in water. Some bases can be found around your home, and like acids, they may be weak or

d You Know?

r stomach makes
very strong acid,
lled hydrochloric
d, to help digest
our food. Why
sn't it burn you?
stomach lining is
ted with a thick
 of gooey mucus,
h protects it from
act with the acid.

Many household cleaners are solutions made of bases. Mild bases, such as soap, feel slippery because of the way they react with the oils on our skin. Strong bases are very corrosive.

strong. Weak bases include baking soda and soaps—things we use to clean ourselves and our clothes. Strong bases, such as oven cleaners and drain cleaners, can be harmful. They can actually burn or eat away your skin.

What happens if you mix an acid and a base together? The two substances react and cancel each other out. After the reaction, if the right amounts of acid and base were used, the solution is neither acidic nor basic. Only water, salt, and possibly other chemicals are left. The solution has been neutralized. It has no overall charge.

Scientists use a pH scale to measure how acidic or basic

Neutralizing the Pain

You can ease the pain of an ant bite with a simple acid-base reaction. The poison in the bite is an acid. So you can neutralize the pain by using baking soda, a basic compound that reacts with the acid. Baking soda works on bee stings too, but meat tenderizer is even better. The poison in a bee sting is acidic, but it also contains dozens of other chemicals, including proteins. Meat tenderizer breaks down proteins and therefore destroys the poison.

a liquid is. On a scale from 0 to 14, acids are found between 0 and 7. Pure water has a pH of 7 because it is neutral. Bases have a pH between 7 and 14. The liquids you drink have a pH of 7 or a little below or above that mark. But the pH of chemicals in a laboratory can range from less than 1 (very strong acids, such as the sulfuric acid in a car battery) all the way up to 14 (strong bases, such as the lye in drain cleaners). The chemicals at both ends of the pH scale are very dangerous.

Acid Rain

Every year, tons of chemicals are sent into the atmosphere as factories, power plants, automobiles, and homes burn fuels for energy. These chemicals include sulfur dioxide and nitrogen oxides, which cause a kind of air pollution called acid rain. When it rains, snows, or sleets, the sulfur dioxide and nitrogen oxides in the atmosphere dissolve in the water droplets and produce very powerful acids. As this acid rain falls to Earth's surface, it seeps into the ground, as well as into lakes and rivers, killing fish, plants, and wildlife. Scientists have been working hard to try to solve the acid rain problem. For example, they have developed devices that remove sulfur and nitrogen compounds from fuels before they get into the atmosphere.

Not Just for Atoms

What happens if you carefully mix a solution of hydrochloric acid (HCl) in water with a solution of a salt called sodium sulfide (Na_2S)? Phew, what a stink! You have made hydrogen sulfide (H_2S), a gas with the odor of rotten eggs. The hydrogen from the acid has taken the place of the sodium in the salt. The equation for this reaction is:

$$2HCl + Na_2S \rightarrow H_2S + 2NaCl$$

As you can see from this example, chemical reactions are not just simple combinations of one element with another. They can be quite complicated. Atoms can react with molecules, and molecules can react with other molecules in many different ways.

For example, how do you make carbon dioxide gas? One way is to burn carbon ($C + O_2 \rightarrow CO_2$). Another way is to add an acid to baking soda ($NaHCO_3$, a white powder that is also called sodium bicarbonate). This reaction is used to produce carbon dioxide in fire extinguishers. As you might guess from its name, baking soda can also be used in baking to produce bubbles that make dough and batter rise.

In a fire extinguisher, a liquid acid and solid base, sodium bicarbonate, are brought into contact. They react to form carbon dioxide. This gas is heavier than air and puts out the fire by preventing oxygen from getting to it.

Modern chemists design and carry out reactions that are far more complicated than these. Some of them involve dozens of chemicals and hundreds of steps. They may be run on automated machines controlled by computers. Such machines are used, for example, to build, or synthesize, proteins and DNA molecules containing thousands of atoms, similar to those made by living things.

What Makes Reactions Go?

If you put any two compounds together, will you get a reaction? Possibly, but probably not. If they are both dry powders, they will very likely just sit there doing nothing. But add water, and you may see some action. Although the water itself never actually reacts, it is often necessary to get a reaction going. This is because many compounds dissolve in water. This helps separate the ions in ionic compounds so they can move around and find new partners.

Dissolving chemical compounds in water is just one way of getting two substances to react. Often they *can* react but will not unless they are given a little push in the right direction. Putting in some energy is a way to get reactions started. Heating a mixture or solution is one common method. It may not take much heat, and in fact, once the reaction gets going, it may give out a lot more heat than it took in. When you are starting a fire in a fireplace, for example, you start it off with something that burns easily, such as newspaper. The burning newspaper heats up the logs in the fireplace until finally the logs start to burn too. Their reaction gives off a lot more heat—enough to warm the whole room.

Other forms of energy, such as light and electricity, can also make chemicals react. Strong sunlight can make the bright colors fade in printed photographs, curtains, or clothes. The light starts up chemical reactions between the colorful dyes and oxygen from the air. Light-absorbing compounds are added to modern dyes in these materials to protect them from fading.

If an electric current is sent through a solution of silver salts, the salts break down chemically, and metallic silver separates out. (That is how a shiny coating of silver is applied to silver-plated forks, spoons, and knives.) High pressure may also give the needed boost to chemical reactions. For example, gases such as hydrogen and nitrogen, which would not normally react with each other, combine to form ammonia under high pressure.

Once a reaction is going, it may continue until all the reacting chemicals are used up. Or it may stop at some point, producing a mixture of both starting materials and products. A reaction is most likely to go all the way if one of the products is removed. Many reaction products form solids that do not dissolve in water and settle to the bottom. In other reactions, a gas is formed and goes off into the air or is sent through a tube to a collecting container.

Some reactions are started off and nudged in the right direction by helper chemicals called catalysts. A catalyst may make a compound more reactive. Or it may grab hold of substances and line them up so that they are in just the right positions to join together. After the reaction is finished, the products may leave the catalyst or be removed. Then the catalyst is as good as new, ready to work on more raw materials. It is not changed by the reaction, even though the reaction could not have happened without it.

Catalysts are used in making various products, such as gasoline and plastics. Catalysts are even more important in the bodies of living organisms. The high temperatures and pressures used in factories would be no good for your body—they would kill you! But catalysts can make reactions go at your own body's temperature. Special proteins called enzymes act as catalysts in the reactions you use to digest your food, build bones and muscles, and even think and dream.

Some Familiar Reactions

Some chemical reactions happen very quickly. When you strike a match, for example, the oxygen in the air bonds quickly to the chemicals in the match head. Striking the match against a matchbook produces friction, which creates heat and kick-starts the reaction. This type of chemical change is called combustion, in which the burning flame gives off heat and light.

Burning a log is also combustion, but it goes more slowly. The wood contains various compounds that contain carbon and hydrogen. When these burn—that is, combine with oxygen from the air—they form carbon dioxide and water.

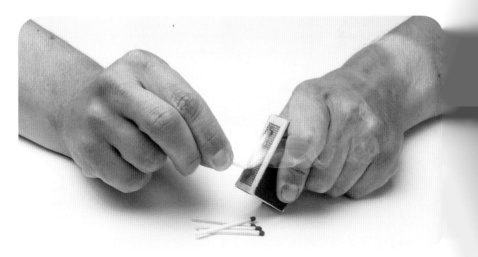

Friction provides the heat that starts the chemical reaction of burning.

(The water doesn't put out the fire because it is produced in very small amounts at a time, and the heat of the fire turns it into steam. So it goes off into the air without your noticing it.)

Some chemical reactions can take weeks, months, or even years to happen. Have you ever seen a rusty old car sitting in a junkyard? Brownish red patches appear all over the car. If you tried to clean the rust off, you would wind up with holes in the metal. It seems almost as if something has been eating the car body away, as if some of the metal "disappeared."

What happened? This old car has probably sat outside in the rain and snow for months or even

Here's a photo of an old, rusted car (**left**) *and a close-up of rust* (**right**). *Rust results when iron combines with oxygen.*

years. Under these damp conditions, iron atoms in the car body combine with oxygen atoms from the air that have dissolved in the water. (Normally, the paint that covers the metal body of a car acts as protection from the rain. But a deep scratch in the paint or dents to the car leave the metal underneath unprotected against the weather.) Chemists use the term *oxidation* for reactions in which metals or other substances combine with oxygen.

The chemical compound that is formed in this case is iron oxide, which is another name for rust. If you scrape off the rust, you are removing some of the iron—that's how you get a hole. Rust is a brand new substance created by a chemical reaction. But unlike the chemical change that creates a flame when you light a match, iron can take a very long time to "burn" and form rust.

Metals such as copper, brass, and silver are normally bright, shiny substances. They can be made into very attractive products, such as jewelry, silverware, pots, and collectibles. But chemical reactions can cause these metals to tarnish, or discolor, losing their bright, shiny

Did You Know?
Unlike iron and some of the other metals, aluminum does not rust. The outer surface of an aluminum part reacts with oxygen in the air, just as iron does, but the compound that is formed (aluminum oxide) does not crumble away. It is actually *harder and stronger* than aluminum itself and forms a protective coating.

This close-up of tarnished silver shows the dark patches of silver sulfide that form when the silver is exposed to the air.

luster. Silver, for example, will go through chemical reactions when it is exposed to sulfur-containing compounds in the air, in food, or in skin oils. The silver combines with sulfur to form silver sulfide, which is the dark-colored tarnish found on silver. (The tarnish on silver may look like a combination of purple, blue, and black.) If you remove the silver sulfide with silver polish (a mixture containing acid), the silver will be bright and shiny again. But you will lose a little silver each time you polish the silverware.

Supersized Molecules

As you know, water is a simple compound, which contains only three atoms—two hydrogen atoms and one oxygen atom. But some molecules are much larger and may contain hundreds or even thousands of atoms. Often these molecules are formed by linking together a lot of small molecules, such as ethylene (H_2CCH_2), to form long chains. Such supersized molecules are called polymers (meaning "many parts").

Some polymers are formed naturally, in the cells of animals and plants. For example, plants link small sugar molecules into chains to form two different kinds of polymers: starch, which is a carbohydrate that our bodies can use as food, and cellulose, a tough polymer carbohydrate that we cannot digest. Plant leaves and stems, such as broccoli and spinach, contain a lot of cellulose. Proteins, which build our body structures, are polymers made of amino acids. DNA, the chemical that stores the instructions for our cells and bodies, is a polymer too.

Did You Know?
Bacteria in a cow's stomach can digest cellulose, breaking it down into sugars. That's why cows can eat grass, hay, and other plant matter as food.

These spinach leaves and stems are mostly cellulose, or plant fiber. We can get some nutrients from spinach, but we don't have the right enzymes to digest cellulose.

Some polymers are made in laboratories and factories. The most common types are plastics. Many different kinds of plastics are produced. How they form depends on the type of molecules that react with one another. One type of plastic that you probably have around the house is plastic wrap. Plastic wrap is thin and flexible. Another kind of molecule that forms long polymer chains produces a hard plastic, such as a comb or plastic containers. The foam rubber padding in mattresses and cushions is another kind of plastic, formed with a light, spongy texture.

Digestion Reactions

We have seen how chemical reactions happen in laboratories and factories. But do you know that important chemical reactions are happening in your own body all the time? In fact, you can't live without them. For example, your body needs energy for everything you do. You use energy when you run around with your friends, work on your computer, or even sleep. Energy is needed so that your muscles can move, your heart can beat, and your lungs can breathe. You get this energy from the food you eat.

Food contains chemicals, called nutrients, that our bodies need to grow and stay healthy. But foods have to go through some big changes before our bodies can use the nutrients they contain. Even the tiniest crumb is too big to fit into the cells of your

Skating and skateboarding use up lots of energy. These boys will probably be hungry when they get home!

body. And the chemicals in food are too complex for the cells to handle. Usually they must be broken down into simpler building blocks. The process of breaking down foods into smaller bits that can be used by the body is called digestion.

Digestion involves a series of chemical reactions. The first reaction starts in your mouth. When you take a bite out of a sandwich, for example, the food mixes with watery saliva. Saliva contains digestive enzymes, which are chemicals that start breaking the bonds of some of the food molecules. After the food is swallowed, it travels down to the stomach, where acid and more enzymes react with it and break down the food molecules even further.

The pancreas and the liver release more digestive enzymes to break down the food. Inside the small intestine, enzymes

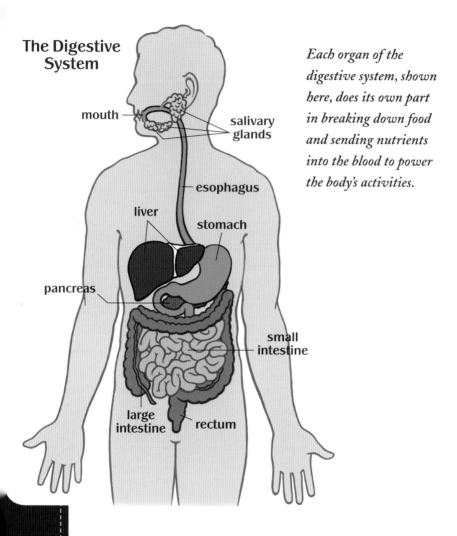

The Digestive System

Each organ of the digestive system, shown here, does its own part in breaking down food and sending nutrients into the blood to power the body's activities.

mouth

salivary glands

esophagus

liver

stomach

pancreas

small intestine

large intestine

rectum

help to turn most of the food into a liquid. The nutrients are now small enough to pass through the walls of the small intestine and into the blood. The blood carries the food materials to all the body cells to be used as energy to power their activities. What is not used by the body passes out of the large intestine as waste.

Plant Reactions

Like humans and other animals, plants need food for energy. But plants do not eat. They make their own food through a process called photosynthesis. Photosynthesis, as its name suggests, uses sunlight energy (the *photo* part of the word) to put simple chemicals together to form more complex chemicals (a *synthesis*).

During photosynthesis, the Sun's energy powers a series of chemical reactions. Carbon dioxide from the air and water from the soil are turned into sugars, starches, and other carbohydrates. Green plants get their color from chlorophyll, a green pigment that traps the sunlight energy that makes these reactions go.

Using sunlight energy captured by chlorophyll, plants combine carbon dioxide from the air with water from the soil. The chemical reactions of photosynthesis produce sugars such as glucose. The sugar may be "burned" for energy, stored as starch, or changed into other plant chemicals.

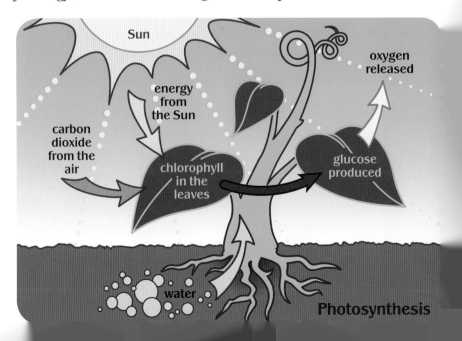

Sun

energy from the Sun

oxygen released

carbon dioxide from the air

chlorophyll in the leaves

glucose produced

water

Photosynthesis

Did You Know?

Plants can photosynthesize only during the day or under artificial lights. If a plant is left in a dark room, the chlorophyll cannot get energy to start a reaction. Then the leaves will wither and eventually the plant will die.

In photosynthesis, plants release oxygen into the air as a by-product. In fact, the oxygen that we breathe is generated from this process. Scientists believe that there was no oxygen gas in Earth's atmosphere until the first plantlike organisms appeared and began producing it about four billion years ago. Here is the basic chemical reaction of photosynthesis, which produces carbohydrates and oxygen from carbon dioxide and water:

$$CO_2 + H_2O + light \rightarrow carbohydrates + O_2$$

Breath of Life

A person could survive without food for up to about two months. But after just four minutes without air, brain cells start to die. We must breathe to live.

With each breath we draw air into our lungs. Oxygen from the air passes from the tiny air sacs in the lungs into the bloodstream and is delivered to all the body cells. In the cells, this vital gas is used to generate energy by reactions with food chemicals. These nutrients contain carbon and hydrogen. Reacting with oxygen converts them to carbon dioxide and water, and energy is released for the body's needs.

The blood carries the carbon dioxide away from the cells to the lungs, where it is breathed out into the air. This whole process, from breathing in oxygen to its energy-producing reactions in the body cells and getting rid of carbon dioxide wastes, is called cellular respiration. Its basic chemical equation is:

$$\text{Carbon-hydrogen chemicals} + O_2 \rightarrow CO_2 + H_2O + \text{heat}$$

This equation is the opposite of photosynthesis. Actually, the carbon dioxide that humans and other animals breathe out is one of the main sources that plants use for photosynthesis.

Matter and "Spaceship Earth"

Our planet came equipped with a whole periodic table of matter. We have learned to use these rich resources for food, shelter, and entertainment. But these resources are limited. Like a spaceship traveling through the galaxy, we have just the supplies we brought with us. If we run out of them, there is nowhere to get more.

There is still plenty for us, for our children, and perhaps for our grandchildren too. But future generations may have trouble finding enough fuel, minerals,

Did You Know?

Plants "breathe" too. In fact, respiration goes on in both plants and animals, all through the day and night. Just like animals, plants take in oxygen from the air and release carbon dioxide. But during the daytime, they give off much more oxygen than they take in. So plants replace the oxygen that people and other living things use up.

and other resources. Often, disposable cameras, cell phones, and old video-game cartridges are thrown in the trash. But our throwaway society will soon have to start changing its ways.

In the future, people will need to use our trash as a resource for making new products. The recycling of newspapers, aluminum cans, and plastics is just a beginning. We need to turn more of our throwaways into useful products. For example, worn-out automobile tires are being used to build reefs and barriers to protect beaches and harbors and provide homes for water wildlife. They are cut up to make rubber sandals and mats and shredded or ground

People have brought old computers, TVs, and electronic waste to this recycling drop-off point in Encino, California.

This bench is made from 100 percent recycled plastic, or Plaswood. This material looks like wood but is much more durable.

to form road surfaces, sidewalks, tiles and bricks, and shock-absorbing paving for playgrounds.

Supplies of metals are likely to become scarce. Future generations will need to use the knowledge of chemistry and physics to make substitutes or work out other ways of doing things. Plastics are already substituting for metals in many products, including cars, trucks, and jet airplanes. The plastics are lighter than the metals they replaced and therefore cut down on the amount of fuel needed. Plastics are also replacing metals in the cases of laptop computers, fishing rods, racquet frames, and the bodies of stringed instruments. Recycled plastic lumber is a woodlike product that can substitute for concrete, wood, and metals in products like fences, walkways, flooring, roofs, and playground equipment.

Our working knowledge of matter and what it can do will continue to grow. It is our best hope for making life easier, safer, and more enjoyable.

Glossary

acid: a substance with a sour taste that can react with a base to form a salt. Acids have a pH of less than 7 and can transfer a proton to a base or accept a pair of electrons from a base.

acid rain: precipitation of acid-forming chemicals (sulfur dioxide and nitrogen oxides) from the atmosphere in rain, snow, or as solid particles

alchemist: a scientist whose goal was to turn other metals, such as lead, into gold. Alchemy is a philosophy that dates back to the Middle Ages (500 to 1500).

alloy: a mixture of different metals

amalgam: an alloy of mercury with another metal or metals

amorphous solids: solids in which atoms and molecules are jumbled together randomly, without forming any regular pattern. Examples are plastics and glass.

atomic number: the number of protons in an atom's nucleus

atomic weight: the total number of protons and neutrons in an atom's nucleus

atoms: tiny particles that are the building blocks of chemical elements. They cannot be broken into smaller particles by chemical reactions.

base: a bitter-tasting substance that can react with an acid to form a salt. Bases have a pH greater than 7 and can accept a proton or give up a pair of electrons to an acid.

boiling point: the temperature at which a liquid turns into a gas

buckyball: a form of solid carbon consisting of sixty carbon atoms, joined into a sphere formed from interlocking hexagons and pentagons

catalyst: a substance that starts, directs, or speeds up a chemical reaction without itself being chemically changed

cellular respiration: the release of energy in living organisms by combining food materials with oxygen

cellulose: a tough polymer carbohydrate composed of sugar units and found in plant cells

chlorophyll: a green pigment in plant cells that traps light energy

combustion: burning; a fast chemical reaction that uses oxygen to produce heat and light

compound: a substance formed by the chemical joining of two or more different atoms to form molecules

condensation: a change of state of matter from liquid to solid or gas to liquid

covalent bond: the joining of two atoms by sharing electrons

crystal: a solid in which atoms and molecules are joined together in a regular pattern, forming flat sheets, cubes, or 3-D structures. Examples are diamonds, salt, and sugar.

decay: the breakdown of an unstable atom into smaller particles

density: the amount (mass) of matter in a unit of volume

deposition: the change of a gas directly into a solid without passing through the liquid state

deuterium: a form of hydrogen containing one proton and one neutron in the nucleus of each atom; also called heavy hydrogen

digestion: the chemical process by which foods are broken down into smaller parts that the body can use

electric field: the space around a charged particle that is affected by the electric charge

electron: a negatively charged particle that moves around the nucleus of an atom or can move freely through an electrical conductor

electrophilic: pertaining to atoms or molecules that accept electrons in forming an ionic bond

elements: the simplest chemical substances, consisting of atoms of all the same kind

enzymes: proteins that affect chemical reactions, acting as catalysts

evaporation: a change of state of matter from liquid to gas

freezing point: the temperature at which a liquid turns into a solid

gas: a state of matter with no definite size or shape. Molecules in a gas are very spread apart and bounce around rapidly and against one another.

insulation: a nonconducting material (such as plastic) that prevents or reduces the transfer of heat, electricity, or sound

ion: an electrically charged particle formed from an atom or molecule

ionic bond: the joining of two atoms with opposite charges, in which electrons are given up by one atom and taken by the other

isotopes: forms of an element with the same atomic number but different atomic weights

liquefaction: the change of a solid or gas into a liquid

liquid: a state of matter with no definite shape. It can take the form of its container, and it flows. Molecules in a liquid are close together but can move around somewhat.

mass: the amount of matter of a substance or object, which resists being moved

matter: anything that has a definite amount of mass and takes up space

melting point: the temperature at which a solid turns into a liquid

mixture: a combination of two or more substances that can be separated by physical means

molecules: the building blocks of matter, consisting of atoms joined by chemical bonds

nanotube: a tube about one-billionth of a meter wide, formed by carbon atoms with a fullerene (buckyball) structure

neutralize: to make a solution neutral, having no overall electrical charge

neutron: a particle with no electrical charge, found in the nucleus of an atom

nuclear reaction: the breakdown or joining together of atomic nuclei, forming nuclei of a different kind and releasing energy (radiation)

nucleophilic: atoms or molecules that give away electrons to their partners in an ionic bond

nucleus: the center of an atom, the nucleus contains protons and neutrons

nutrients: chemicals in food that are used by the body for its various functions

oxidation: reactions in which metals or other substances combine with oxygen; also, reactions in which electrons are removed, or the positive charge of an element is increased

pH: a measure of the hydrogen ion concentration in a solution. The pH ranges from 0 to 14 and decreases when the hydrogen ion concentration increases.

photosynthesis: the chemical process by which plants turn carbon dioxide and water into sugars and starches, using the energy from sunlight

polar covalent bond: a type of covalent bond in which electrons are shared unequally, giving one end a slight positive charge and the other a slight negative charge

polymer: a very large molecule made by joining many smaller molecules together. Examples are starch, cellulose, proteins, DNA, and plastics such as polyethylene and polyurethane.

product: the substance that is formed as a result of chemicals reacting

protium: a form of hydrogen containing only one proton in the nucleus

proton: a positively charged particle found in the nucleus of an atom

radioactive: referring to an atom whose nucleus tends to decay (break down), forming a new isotope or element and releasing radiations

radioactivity: the breakdown of an unstable atomic nucleus, releasing radiation

reactant: the chemical that is reacting

semiconductor: an element or compound that carries electricity at low temperatures but not at high temperatures

solid: a state of matter that has a definite size and shape. The molecules of a solid are packed tightly together.

solution: a homogeneous (uniform) mixture that will not separate when left alone

synthesize: to form by combining parts or elements

tarnish: to dull or discolor a metal substance through chemical reactions

tritium: a form of hydrogen containing one proton and two neutrons in the nucleus of each atom

vacuum: a volume that contains no matter

valence electron: an electron in the outer shell of an atom that can be given to or shared with another atom to form a chemical bond

volume: the amount of space a substance or object takes up

water vapor: water in a gaseous state

Source Notes

44   Peter Van der Krogt. "Hydrogenium/Hydrogen," *Elementymology & Elements Multidict,* May 5, 2005, http://www.vanderkrogt.net/elements/elem/h.html (March 11, 2008).

45   Ibid.

Bibliography

American Chemical Society. "Joseph Priestley: Discoverer of Oxygen." *National Historical Chemical Landmarks.* 2007. http://acswebcontent .acs.org/landmarks/landmarks/priestley/rebel.html (March 12, 2008).

Ball, Philip. *The Ingredients: A Guided Tour of the Elements.* New York: Oxford University Press, 2003.

CCI. "How to Care for . . . Silver." *Canadian Conservation Institute (CCI): Preserving My Heritage.* May 16, 2002. http://www.preservation .gc.ca/howto/articles/silver_e.asp (March 6, 2008).

Cobb, Cathy, and Monty L. Fetterolf. *The Joy of Chemistry: The Amazing Science of Familiar Things.* New York: Prometheus Books, 2005.

eNotes.com. "Energy: Why Was Lead Added to Gasoline and Why Is Lead-Free Gasoline Used in New Cars?" *eNotes.com.* 2006. http:// www.enotes.com/science-fact-finder/energy/why-was-lead-added -gasoline-why-lead-free-gasoline (March 10, 2008).

EPA. "Acid Rain." *U.S. Environmental Protection Agency.* June 8, 2007. http://www.epa.gov/acidrain/#what (March 3, 2008).

———. "Management of Scrap Tires." *U.S. Environmental Protection Agency.* September 7, 2007. http://www.epa.gov/garbage/tires/science .htm (March 10, 2008).

Heilprin, John. Associated Press. "Ozone-Friendly Chemicals Lead to Warming." *Climate Ark News Archive.* August 20, 2006. http://www .climateark.org/shared/reader/welcome.aspx?linkid=59643&keybold =ozone (March 10, 2008).

Plasma TV Science. "The Plasma behind the Plasma TV Screen," *Plasma TV Science.org.* N.d. http://www.plasmatvscience.org/theinnerworkings .html (March 10, 2008).

———. "What Is Plasma?" *Plasma TV Science.org.* N.d. http://www .plasmatvscience.org/whatisplasma.html (March 10, 2008).

Royal Society of Chemistry. "History of the Periodic Table: Dmitri Mendeleev." *LearnNet.* N.d. http://www.chemsoc.org/networks/ learnnet/periodictable/pre16/develop/mendeleev.htm (March 4, 2008).

Shakhashiri, Bassam Z. "Buckyballs." *Chemical of the Week.* November 2007. http://scifun.chem.wisc.edu/chemweek/ buckball/buckball.html (March 10, 2008).

Stwertka, Albert. *A Guide to the Elements.* New York: Oxford University Press, 2002.

Suplee, Curt. *New Everyday Science Explained: From the Big Bang to the Human Genome . . . and Everything In-Between.* Washington, DC: National Geographic Society Press, 2004.

Thomson Gale. "Hydrogen." *World of Scientific Discovery.* 2005–2006. Available online at http://www.bookrags.com/ research/hydrogen-wsd/#bro_copy (March 12, 2008).

Van der Krogt, Peter. "Hydrogenium/Hydrogen." *Elementymology & Elements Multidict.* May 5, 2005. http:// www.vanderkrogt.net/elements/elem/h.html (March 11, 2008).

For Further Information

Books

Ballard, Carol. *Science Answers: Solids, Liquids, and Gases from Ice Cubes to Bubbles.* Chicago: Heinemann Library, 2004.

Baxter, Roberta. *Chemical Reaction.* Farmington Hills, MI: KidHaven Press, 2005.

Cooper, Christopher. *Matter.* New York: DK Publishing, 1999.

Dingle, Adrian. *The Periodic Table: Elements with Style.* New York: Kingfisher Publications, 2007.

Fleisher, Paul. *Liquids and Gases.* Minneapolis: Twenty-First Century Books, 2002.

———. *Matter and Energy.* Minneapolis: Twenty-First Century Books, 2002.

Gardner, Robert. *Science Projects about Solids, Liquids, and Gases.* Berkeley Heights, NJ: Enslow Publishers, 2000.

Juettner, Bonnie. *Molecules.* Farmington Hills, MI: KidHaven Press, 2005.

Miller, Ron. *The Elements: What You Really Want to Know.* Minneapolis: Twenty-First Century Books, 2005.

Stille, Darlene R. *Chemical Change: From Fireworks to Rust.* Minneapolis: Compass Point Books, 2006.

Tocci, Salvatore. *Experiments with Solids, Liquids, and Gases.* New York: Children's Press, 2001.

Vogt, Gregory L. *The Atmosphere.* Minneapolis: Twenty-First Century Books, 2007.

Websites

Kitchen Chemistry
http://pbskids.org/zoom/games/kitchenchemistry/virtual-start.html
Take the challenge on the PBS Kids website. Find the clues to solve the pantry puzzle and do virtual experiments on cabbage juice and a cork rocket to learn about acids and bases and gas under pressure.

Learn about Chemicals around Your House
    http://www.epa.gov/kidshometour/
    Sponsored by the Environmental Protection Agency, this
    website gives you a virtual tour through each room of your
    house, as well as the backyard. What kinds of chemicals
    would you find there? Look around, and you will find them
    and learn about their chemical properties.

Matter and Energy
    http://www.kidskonnect.com/MatterandEnergy/
    MatterEnergyHome.html
    This website includes information and activities about
    "The Atoms Family," including phases of matter, atomic
    structure, and molecules. Other links give information on
    energy, light, and electricity.

Matter: What Are the Building Blocks of the Universe?
    http://www.brainpop.com/science/matter/
    A kid-friendly site with a well-rounded treatment of matter
    includes links with information on atoms, acids and bases,
    compounds and mixtures, crystals, chemical equations, ions,
    matter-changing states, metals, periodic table of elements,
    and more!

Rader's CHEM4KIDS
    http://www.chem4kids.com/
    This site offers an introduction to chemistry for kids
    and everybody, including information on matter, atoms,
    elements, the periodic table, reactions, and biochemistry. It
    includes lots of real-world examples.

Strange Matter
    http://www.strangematterexhibit.com/
    This website includes movies, games, and interactive
    pages on materials science, with the motto: "Discover the
    secrets of everyday stuff." Find out about inner structure,
    transformations, strength of materials (the crusher), and
    improvements; fun stuff for kids, families, and teachers.

Index

Photo Acknowledgments

The images in this book are used with the permission of: © Rob Walls/ Alamy, p. 5; © Bettmann/CORBIS, p. 8; © SuperStock, Inc./SuperStock, p. 13; © Marta Johnson, pp. 15, 23, 81, 91; © Royalty-Free/CORBIS, p.16 (left); © iStockphoto.com/Claudio Baldini, p. 16 (top right); © iStockphoto.com/Christine Balderas, p. 16 (bottom right); © Marek Kosmal/Dreamstime.com, p. 19; © iStockphoto.com/Anton Zhukov, p. 26; © Michel Roggo/naturepl.com, p. 27; © Farhad J Parsa/Photonica/Getty Images, p. 29; © Andrew Lambert Photography/Photo Researchers, Inc., pp. 37, 58; © Russell Kightley/Photo Researchers, Inc., p. 38; © Roger Hagadone/SuperStock, p. 39; © Pictorial Press Ltd/Alamy, p. 46; Library of Congress (LC-USZ62-64936), p. 48; © The Print Collector/Alamy, p. 50; © iStockphoto.com/MH, p. 53; © Photodisc/Getty Images, pp. 63, 88 (right); AP Photo, p. 64; © J. Bernholc et al., NCSU/Photo Researchers, Inc., p. 72; © Jeffrey Coolidge/The Image Bank/Getty Images, p. 83; © Clive Streeter/Dorling Kindersley/Getty Images, p. 87; © Richard Cummins/SuperStock, p. 88 (left); © David Cavagnaro/Visuals Unlimited, p. 90; © Photononstop/SuperStock, p. 93; © Robyn Beck/AFP/Getty Images, p. 98; © Mark Boulton/Alamy, p. 99. Illustrations by © Laura Westlund/Independent Picture Service, pp. 12, 21, 33, 35, 36, 94, 95; © Bill Hauser/Independent Picture Service, pp. 52, 57, 62, 66, 69, 71, 76.

Front cover: © Paul Taylor/The Image Bank/Getty Images.

About the Authors

Dr. Alvin Silverstein is a former professor of biology and director of the physician assistant program at the College of Staten Island of the City University of New York. Virginia B. Silverstein is a translator of Russian scientific literature.

The Silversteins' collaboration began with a biochemical research project at the University of Pennsylvania. Since then they have produced six children and more than two hundred published books that have received high acclaim for their clear, timely, and authoritative coverage of science and health topics.

Laura Silverstein Nunn, a graduate of Kean College, began helping with the research for her parents' books while she was in high school. Since joining the writing team, she has coauthored more than eighty books.